ABERDEENSHIRE
LIBRARIES

WITHDRAWN
FROM LIBRARY

ABERDEENSHIRE
LIBRARIES

Tim Wonnacott
Moneymaking Antiques
for the Future

ABERDEENSHIRE
LIBRARIES

WITHDRAWN
FROM LIBRARY

ABERDEENSHIRE
LIBRARIES

WITHDRAWN
FROM LIBRARY

ABERDEENSHIRE
LIBRARIES
WITHDRAWN
FROM LIBRARY

ABERDEENSHIRE
LIBRARIES

WITHDRAWN
FROM LIBRARY

ABERDEENSHIRE
LIBRARIES

WITHDRAWN
FROM LIBRARY

ABERDEENSHIRE
LIBRARIES

WITHDRAWN
FROM LIBRARY

ABERDEENSHIRE
LIBRARIES

A L I S
1486549

Tim Wonnacott's
Moneymaking
Antiques for the Future

First published in Great Britain in 2004 by Virgin Books Ltd,
Thames Wharf Studios, Rainville Road, London W6 9HA

Copyright © Tim Wonnacott 2004

The right of Tim Wonnacott to be identified as the Author
of this Work has been asserted by him in accordance with
the Copyright, Designs and Patents Act, 1988.

This book is sold subject to the condition that it shall not, by way of trade
or otherwise, be lent, resold, hired out or otherwise circulated without the
publisher's prior written consent in any form of binding or cover other than
that in which it is published and without a similar condition including
this condition being imposed on the subsequent purchaser.

A catalogue record for this book is available from the British Library.

ISBN 0 7535 0916 4

Designed and typeset by Smith & Gilmour, London
Print and Bound in Italy

Wonnacott, Tim

Tim Wonnacott's
moneymaking
antiques for
                    745.
                     1

1486549

PICTURE CREDITS

Christie's Images Ltd: 19, 20(l), 20(r), 28, 26, 29(l), 29(r), 30, 40(l), 42, 47, 60(l), 61,
62(b), 64(t), 64(b), 90, 91(t), 91(b), 92, 93, 95(t), 95(b), 96, 97(t), 122(tr), Sotheby's Picture
Library: 18, 26(r), 31(b), 45, 50, 51, 52(l), 52(r), 53, 55, 56(l), 56(r), 59, 60(r), 62(t), 68(r), 70,
113, 114, 115, 116, 117, 118, 119(t), 119(b), 122(tl), 122(b), 123, 125(b), David Battie: 74(l),
74(tr), 74(br), 76, 77, 78, 79(l), 79(r), 80(t), 80(b), N. Bloom & Son: 129(t), 129(b), 130(t),
130(b), 132(t), 132(c), 132(b), 134(t), 134(c), 134(b), Bonhams: 10, 16(b), 99, 100(t), 100(b),
101, 102, 103,104(r), James Strang: 82(t), 82(b), 83, 84, 85, 86, 87, 88(t), 88(b), Adam Hills:
106, 107(t), 107(b), 109(l), 109(t), 109(b), 111(t), Tim Wonnacott: 8, 11, 12, 13, 15, 104(l),
Madeleine Marsh: 67, 68, 69, 71, 72(t), Jonathan Clark & Co., London: 137, 138(t), 138(b),
139(b), 143(t), Corbis: 43, 48(l), 60, 121, The Maas Gallery Ltd, London: 139(tr), 138(r),
140, 141, Marc Allum: 35, 36, Nigel Williams: 124, 127(r), James Morton, Morton &
Eden: 9, Louise Irvine: 16(t), British Vintage Radio Museum: 17, Sheffield Railwayana
Auctions: 31(t), Laura Cohn: 34, Ericsson archives (Centre for Business History,
Stockholm): 37, Motorola, Inc., 2004: 38, Jim Forte, www.postalhistory.com: 39,
Sowden Design: 40(r), Lars Tharp: 44, San Francisco Museum of Modern Art/© Jeff
Koons: 47, www.talkingpresidents.com: 48(r), Lulu Guinness: 72, Deborah Strutt: 97(b),
Hansgrohe: 111(b), Clive Farahar and Sophie dupré: 125(t), Express Newspapers: 127(l),
Garton & Co., London: 139(tl), Celia Stolper: 143(b)

KEY TO PICTURE LOCATIONS
l – left, r – right, c – centre, t – top, b – bottom, tl – top left, tr – top right, bl – bottom
left, br – bottom right

Every effort has been made to contact copyright holders. If any omissions do occur the
publisher would be delighted to give full credit in subsequent reprints and editions.

CONTENTS

WHO'S WHO IN THE BOOK

DANIEL AGNEW
Daniel joined Christie's South Kensington fifteen years ago, straight from school, his enthusiasm having been inspired by his antique dealer mother. Since 2001 Daniel has headed the Doll and Teddy Bear department, overseeing the sale in 2003 of Dingley Hall for £124,000, the second most expensive doll's house in the world.

MARC ALLUM
Marc, a director of Rosebery's auctioneers in London, has fifteen years' experience of a busy saleroom. Personal favourites include antiquities, Grand Tour items and antique drinking glasses. Marc appears frequently on television and radio, including the *Antiques Roadshow*. He also lectures and writes regularly for publications such as *BBC Homes & Antiques*.

PAUL ATTERBURY
Paul Atterbury is a writer, lecturer, curator and *Antiques Roadshow* expert who specialises in the art and design of the nineteenth and twentieth centuries. A transport enthusiast, he has been excited by trains and railways since he was a small boy, trainspotting on Surbiton station.

DAVID BATTIE
David worked at Sotheby's in the departments of Ceramics and Oriental Works of Art and was appointed a director in 1976. He retired in 1999. His publications have included *The Price Guide to 19th and 20th Century British Pottery* and he is the Editor of *Sotheby's Encyclopaedia of Porcelain*. David, who has appeared on the *Antiques Roadshow* since 1979, makes numerous other radio and television appearances and lectures all over the world.

GRAHAM BUDD
Graham joined Sotheby's from school, moving on to organise Sotheby's first horse racing and football memorabilia sales in 1998. One of his greatest finds was a collection of Manchester City programmes dating back to 1900, subsequently sold for over £50,000. Graham is the author of *Horseracing Art & Memorabilia* and *Soccer Memorabilia*. In 2004 Graham set up Graham Budd Auctions, which conducts sporting memorabilia sales in association with Sotheby's.

CLIVE FARAHAR
Clive started buying books from fêtes and jumble sales at eight years of age. He began his career, and later became a partner, at one of the last great bookselling firms in London, Francis Edwards of Marylebone, whose customers had included Charles Dickens, Thackeray, Pinero, the Barretts of Wimpole Street and royalty. Principally a bookseller and appraiser, Clive also lectures, writes and broadcasts, particularly with the *Antiques Roadshow*.

IAN HARRIS
Ian has 50 years' experience of the silver and jewellery business. Since leaving school he has worked with his family firm, N. Bloom, then antique and Victorian silver dealers, and, since 1969, retail jewellers. Ian is the author of two silver price guides. He worked with Arthur Negus on *Going for a Song* and has done 26 years with the *Antiques Roadshow*. He has been on the advisory board for Olympia, and is a dealer/director of LAPADA, the Association of Art and Antique Dealers.

ADAM HILLS
Adam started Retrouvius Architectural Reclamation and Design in 1993 in Glasgow with partner Maria Speake. In co-operation with building preservation trusts and conservation bodies, they established a market for architectural salvage in the city. Since moving to London in 1997, they have developed their interest in the field, working with designers and architects, and have undertaken their own building projects.

HILARY KAY

Hilary joined Sotheby's after school and, aged 21, became Sotheby's youngest ever auctioneer. When she left Sotheby's in 1999 after 22 years, she was Senior Director and auctioneer running seven expert departments. Now an independent consultant, broadcaster, lecturer and writer on antiques and collectables, Hilary has been an *Antiques Roadshow* expert since 1979 and has featured in many other television and radio programmes, and recently presented BBC1's series *Brilliantly British*. She is the author of *Rock 'n' Roll Collectables – an Illustrated History of Rock Memorabilia*.

RUPERT MAAS

Rupert, an *Antiques Roadshow* regular, owns and runs The Maas Gallery, which deals in Victorian, Pre-Raphaelite, Romantic and Modern British paintings, watercolours, drawings, reproductive engravings and sculpture, and the work of a few living artists. Rupert has held Pre-Raphaelite exhibitions as well as annual exhibitions of Victorian paintings. He lectures, and writes regularly on art.

MADELEINE MARSH

Madeleine has run her own company, researching paintings and antiques for dealers, collectors and auction houses. Her books have included *Art Detective: How to Research Your Paintings, Antiques and Collectables*. General Editor of *Miller's Collectables Price Guide* since 1995, she is currently preparing the 2005 edition. She appears regularly on television and radio, including the *Antiques Roadshow*, writes for magazines and newspapers, and gives lectures.

HENRY SANDON

Curator of Royal Worcester for seventeen years, Henry carried out archaeological excavations on the site of the original factory which made a major contribution to knowledge of early Worcester porcelain. He has written many books on the history of Worcester and other porcelains. He has appeared on both *Going for a Song* and the *Antiques Roadshow*.

JAMES STRANG

A descendant of the distinguished Scottish architect Alexander 'Greek' Thomson, James began a successful career in furniture and lighting design in the 1980s. Through this, his interest developed into a passion for collecting and dealing in twentieth-century design. He has supplied many international collections, specialising in the work of early twentieth-century architect/designers and the British Modernists.

LARS THARP

Born in Copenhagen, Lars was formerly a director and auctioneer with Sotheby's. Since 1993 he has run his own consultancy, advising museums, auction houses and private owners on the acquisition, care and disposal of ceramics. He lectures worldwide. Appearing on television and radio for nearly twenty years, Lars is well known to viewers of the *Antiques Roadshow,* and presents his own series, *Inside Antiques*.

RUPERT VAN DER WERFF

Rupert has worked in the Garden Statuary department at Sotheby's since 1998. In 2000 he qualified for membership of the RICS. He has written books for Miller's and magazine articles on various aspects of the garden antiques trade. He became head of department in 2001 and has recently become a director of Sotheby's.

TIM WONNACOTT

Tim started as a chartered auctioneer in his father's auction business in Devon. After studying at the Victoria and Albert Museum, a spell at the West End auction house Phillips, Son & Neale, and a year in North America, Tim joined Sotheby's. He worked there for 25 years, becoming chairman of Sotheby's Olympia saleroom. He left in 2003 to start his own independent fine art and antiques agency, Tim Wonnacott & Associates, and a television production company, Wonna Productions Ltd., and Tim Wonnacott Media Services. Over the past fifteen years, Tim has appeared regularly on the *Antiques Roadshow*, *The Antiques Show* and *Going Going Gone!* among others. To date, he has presented over 150 *Bargain Hunt* daytime programmes.

INTRODUCTION
WHAT DOES 'MONEYMAKING ANTIQUES' FOR THE FUTURE MEAN?

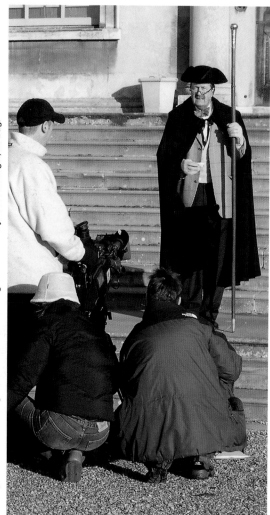

Tim Wonnacott strutting his stuff for *Bargain Hunt* outside the west front of Belton House, near Grantham, Lincolnshire, holding the staff and wearing the cloak and hat of the eighteenth-century house manager, Mr Bug!

Years ago, the definition of an antique was an object 'over 100 years old'. But top class antiques fairs no longer enforce strict datelines, merely insisting an object under 100 years old must be of good enough quality to be worthy of admission. Thus, you find today all manner of high class wares by excellent contemporary craftspeople alongside traditional antiques – a healthy development for the whole business. This redefinition of the word 'antique' has unleashed a gust of fresh air into what was seen as a dry, dusty, elitist world, with arty rituals and unintelligible lingo.

So, having liberated the term 'antique', we have to consider its stable-mate, the term 'collectable' – a wonderful catch-all phrase encompassing almost anything imaginable, because so much is a collectable nowadays.

What this book sets out to do is to outline collecting avenues open to you at the beginning of the 21st century, with each chapter describing moneymaking opportunities from collecting twentieth-century objects. I have chosen the twentieth century as our hunting ground because some pieces will be nearly 100 years old and quite traditional, while others will be equally exciting and nearly brand new. Whatever the reason, throughout the book, there are tips from the experts for potential moneymaking antiques for the future.

THE COLLECTING DISEASE

What is it that spurs collectors on? The prospect of profit? The thrill of the chase? The obsessive desire to acquire a complete set – and the rarer the set, the greater the pleasure?

The archetypal child collector is a boy in shorts avidly ferreting out his stamps, marbles, cigarette cards or, more recently, Pokemon cards, and using every opportunity to swap, scrounge or spend precious pocket money in pursuit of his Holy Grail. This is good news as it helps develop social and economic skills (you need to be able to communicate to barter effectively), and there is no better way for a child to understand the value of money than by handing over scarce cash. If the object bought appreciates in value, the child enjoys a double whammy – pleasure from profit, plus gaining knowledge of the historical and social aspects of a collecting field.

A friend of mine encouraged his seven-year-old son to collect British campaign and gallantry medals. The typical First World War trio of medals was handed out to the millions of combatants and is now cheap as a result. The rarer campaigns also had their medals and the young collector can look up places around the globe, and dream of acts of heroism and gallantry.

Specialist coin and medal dealers Morton & Eden sold Gunner Israel Harding's Victoria Cross the other day (he stuffed a shell with a spluttering fuse into a barrel of water, thereby saving his ship, off Alexandria in July 1882). It made £75,000! Expensive but very rare. Just as desirable, but sold for just £50 in the same sale, was a very fine Khedive's Star, dated 1884, awarded to Lance Sergeant Gregory of the Royal Hussars. Just the job for the youngster's collection and a good way to learn something of the nineteenth-century history of the Middle East.

My theory is that the grown-up collector at heart is no different from that child in shorts. The only difference is that he has the money and determination to realise his yearning to collect. In the 1970s, another friend accurately predicted the extraordinary rise in classic car prices. He reminded me that the post Second World War baby boomers, in their late teens by the late 1950s, would have been lucky to have owned their own moped, let alone a car. So the young moped owner never forgot some Flash Harry in an 'E'-type Jag

The Victoria Cross awarded to Gunner Israel Harding in 1882, sold in December 2003 by Morton & Eden

1965 Jaguar 'E'-type 4.2-litre Fixed Head Coupe. Cost new £1,900. Sold by Bonhams at Goodwood, 2003, for £32,000

whizzing by at 95 mph in 1962, all Brylcreemed and cocooned by chicks. But, by the mid 1980s, the baby-boomer was in his forties and had done well for himself during the Thatcher years. When a restored 'E' type, a vision in testosterone red, appeared for only £27,500 in that month's *Classic Cars* magazine, the deep ache felt all those years before leapt to the fore. Suddenly, Mr Careful (who would never have dreamt of spending £27,500 on a painting) was tempted and had become a collector!

SO HOW DO YOU MAKE MONEY OUT OF ANTIQUES?

As in most walks of life, there is no substitute for experience. If, like me and all my contributors, you have lived and breathed antiques and collectables most of your life, it is easier to spot a bargain and do something about it.

But don't despair. The inexperienced collector simply needs to select a collecting area that really interests him, stoke up some passion and prepare to learn about that area inside out. Going to fairs and car boots and auctions all form part of that educating process. Watching television programmes, buying the book on your chosen subject, trawling the internet for information, looking at opportunities to buy and sell, computing that information, is fun and will help make you into a wizard bargain hunter with an eye for the future!

When making more than 150 *Bargain Hunt* programmes over the past 18 months, I have scoured antiques fairs and auctions up and down the country. Some of the time, I am on camera, strutting my stuff, and also off-camera finding pieces and helping contestants. But, every day, I find time to go looking for things for myself that might make a profit. And most days I have been lucky enough to find some bargain or other. Take this silver pig, a real little 'Pigling Bland'. I spotted him in a box containing twenty or thirty pieces of ceramic and plated junk in an auction. (Country auctioneers often just bundle up odds and ends from house clearance jobs into cardboard boxes.) 'Boxed lot as seen,' shouts the porter when it comes up for sale, the auctioneer asks for £20

the lot and you stick your hand up. If you are lucky and no one else has looked in the box, or if they haven't spotted the sweet little pig (only two and a half inches long and as black as your hat), then the thing is yours!

It is understandable that the auctioneer missed the silver mark for Chester 1912, as it is tiny and just visible above one trotter. More importantly, he also missed, on another trotter, the equally small mark, S M & Co, for the celebrated silversmiths and small workers Sampson Mordan and Co. Started in 1815, the firm's fortune was founded as patentees and makers of the 'ever-pointed pencil and portable pen'. By the time my pig was made in 1912, the firm had branched out into high-class novelties for West End shops like Asprey's, and prospered until an incendiary device destroyed their workshop in 1941. All I had to do was to clean little piggy up and put him on a base. The lovely polished bloodstone plinth cost me nothing because – you got it – the plinth was part of a boxed

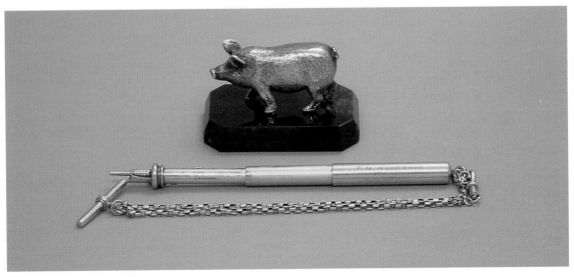

A Sampson Mordan and Co. silver pig, London 1910, and a Mordan gold propelling pencil and chain

An 'indoor' Bargain Hunt fair, Edinburgh, 2003

lot I bought ten years ago (moral: never throw anything away). I have recently had it valued for between £250 and £400! Not bad for £20!

Even better is the propelling pencil in the same photograph. When opened up telescopically, it is nearly six inches long, and was described at the fair where I saw it as 'a gilt metal propelling pencil and chain, 1930, price £18'. I spotted the stamp, S Mordan and Co, and then its two slides, one pushing out a pencil (the famous 'ever pointed') and the other to hold a steel nib. The dealer volunteered to let me have it for £12. The pen

is eighteen carat solid gold (not all small work was hallmarked in the nineteenth century but I have had it tested) and the chain is nine carat solid gold but, again, unmarked. Value? In a sale, one could expect £200 for the pen and £50 or so for the chain, but there is a further excitement concerning the inscription on the pen's outer shaft. Why did the dealer date the thing (incorrectly) as 1930? He obviously thought the inscription, which reads 'Souvenir of F W Wyndham who died April 30th 1930', gave the age of the pen, which it doesn't. What the inscription means is that the pen was bequeathed following the death of Mr Wyndham in 1930, but it could well have been bought by him around 1860. I then asked myself whether, if someone thought it worthwhile paying for an inscription on a second-hand, old-fashioned pen in 1930, was the F. W. Wyndham mentioned famous enough to warrant the effort? A trawl on the internet revealed that my Wyndham was the theatrical impresario partner of Howard and Wyndham Ltd, who put on plays up and down the country between 1895 and 1928. So, my £12 gilt metal pen and chain, made of gold by a celebrated maker, is worth £200 to £250. And, by dint of my researching the inscription, it may well be worth even more to a luvvie collector of theatre-related bibelots. Don't let anyone say that there aren't bargains out there in fairs and auctions!

These are only two examples of the many finds I have recently come across – you simply have to be prepared to look extremely hard and do some research.

However, there are lots of potential pitfalls. Never be ashamed of mistakes you make. We all do it. I stupidly bought a framed group of three E. H. Sheppard drawings of Eeyore, Pooh and Tigger the other day, at a so-called antiques fair in the Midlands. At first glance I got excited, thinking they were worth at least £400 to £600 each and the dealer wanted £20 for the three, which I duly paid. If only I had looked carefully, I would have detected the little dots which are the sign of a printed image. They weren't drawings at all – just mass-produced prints mounted as drawings under a cut board, framed and glazed to deceive. And worth? Precisely £20!

In this book, you will benefit from over 400 years' worth of specialist antiques experience.

My selected authors give you tips and hints based on their experience, to fire up your interest and point you in the right direction. If you have never bought an antique or collectable, I hope each chapter will give you the inspiration to go out there and hunt for these moneymaking antiques for the future.

Good luck and good hunting!

Keep your eye open – you never know what you might find

[1]

TIM WONNACOTT ...
MASTER OF THE MISCELLANEOUS

What's with this miscellaneous lark? Why do I want to write about a lot of oddball objects which don't fit into any normal antiques category? Well, the miscellaneous bit goes back to my first *Antiques Roadshow*. The call came out of the blue from the *Roadshow* production office in Bristol: 'Would I be free to attend a day's filming at Newcastle Emlyn?' I had been working for a dozen years at Sotheby's, was a junior director, and was cataloguing at that time over 6,000 lots of furniture, clocks and watches, bronzes and works of art at the firm's Chester saleroom. I was not going to miss out on this opportunity! I lied and said I was free. It was explained that, as it was a trial, I was coming along just as an observer. Amusing, because they may have called me an 'observer' but all they wanted me there for was to observe *me*!

At the production hotel the night before, I particularly enjoyed my chat with John Bly, the programme's long-term furniture guru, who had a leg in plaster having slipped over walking with Hugh Scully in Cornwall the week before. The next morning, I pitched up at the usual hideous sports hall at 8.30 and was taken aback to see the queue already snaking out of sight! I was hanging about waiting for instructions when word came through that John Bly had sadly been rushed to hospital, having broken his other leg on the hotel steps.

In a flash, from humble observer, I was promoted to the furniture expert (not John's but my lucky break?). All went well for a couple of hours until John Bly re-appeared in a wheelchair with both legs in plaster! Don't let anyone say that things aren't competitive on the *Antiques Roadshow*. Instead, I was asked to help with a big queue that built up at the miscellaneous table – the term applied to any object other experts were not prepared to look at, or didn't know about. Often, the most unusual, problematic and interesting pieces percolated through there.

I discovered a world of shared knowledge inhabited by versatile experts, including Paul Atterbury, Hilary Kay, Marc Allum and Madeline Marsh, all of whom have contributed to this book. No single expert could possibly expect to know everything about everything, particularly when the public sometimes deliberately bring their most obscure and wacky pieces to try to catch us out. Made welcome immediately, I felt I had arrived at the right place at the right time. As a result of that eventful day, I have been happily a 'miscellaneous' expert on the *Roadshow* for fifteen years, without a backwards glance at the more glamorous furniture![1]

An outdoor *Antiques Roadshow* at Dyrham Park near Bath. 2,800 people joined us that day

MONEYMAKING COLLECTABLES OF THE FUTURE

I discussed in the introduction the nature of the collector and the infinite variety of objects for which collectors obsessively hunt. These objects do not need to be antique to be valuable, for age bears no relation to monetary value in the collectables business: it is likely that the twentieth century will prove to be a rich century for sourcing as yet unrecognised moneymaking antiques for the future. The potential for profit out of ordinary objects is incredible. It is just a question of opening one's eyes, understanding the collector's psyche, spotting changing fashions, and getting down to some thorough research!

THE ENDLESS VARIETY OF MODERN COLLECTABLES

On *Bargain Hunt* in Edinburgh, I met David, an Edinburgh University graduate who now works there, and Victoria, a student at the university. I like to get under the skin of the contestants, to discover more about individuals and share surprises with the viewers. After some probing, I discovered that Victoria is a collector on a big scale, which she hadn't admitted when interviewed for the programme. Surprisingly, secretly lurking in this university person's life was a collecting passion for My Little Ponies! She had 1,000 of those rubbery brightly coloured toys made from 1981 in America by Hasbro. David and Victoria have gone

Rare early Bunnykins pieces produced in 1939. Top to bottom, left to right, Mother £1,500; Farmer £1,200; Teapot £750; Mary £1,200; Reggie £2,000; Freddie £2,000 and Billy £1,200

Beswick horse, Spirit of Whitfield, designed by Graham Tongue in 1987 and sold by Bonhams recently for £11,353

"One of three replicas of 'Spirit of Whitfield'. The original was presented to H.R.H. The Princess Royal on the occasion of her visit to Chatterley Whitfield Mining Museum to open the New Pit on October 13th 1987. This model, one of only four cast was sculpted by Graham Tongue, chief designer of the John Beswick studio of Royal Doulton. It is based on 'Kruger' the last pit pony to work at the colliery, who retired in 1931"

around car boots for years picking up My Little Ponies, swapping, buying and selling them. The most valuable is apparently one called Rumplestiltskin which regularly sells for £500 plus. [2]

So, a lesson learned . . . never, ever decry someone else's collecting field or obsessive behaviour, because, before long, you could be behaving in exactly the same way!

The collector as custodian of history is a popular idea, but, for the more obsessive collector, it's just a question of pursuing a subject to the critical mass stage when the sheer numbers take over and start to create value. Consider the 25-year-old ex-milkman who has 5,000 bottles in his shed. His theory is that the milkman is on the way out, and named glass milk bottles will soon be worth something.

Perhaps most incredible of all is Robert Opie, whose collection includes packaging, advertising, toys and games, magazines, postcards and many other layers of consumer social history. Anything that is wrapped, in a package, tin or box, is his quarry. His collection of over 500,000 packaged objects is a valuable resource worth a fortune in its own right. But it also earns its keep because he rents out, for example, the odd packet of Woodbines as an authentic 1920s prop to the movie industry, and period images of packaging for retro advertisements. [3]

Henry Sandon eulogises in his chapter about Royal Worcester, Royal Crown Derby and Wedgwood, but there's a mind-boggling variety of other ceramic moneymaking collectables out there waiting to be discovered.

Take Royal Doulton's Bunnykins wares, conceived as a standard range of nursery china and decorated with frolicking bunnies by Barbara Vernon, the daughter of a Doulton's director. Sold typically as christening presents from 1933, they do not appear on the surface to have much collecting potential. But, shortly after Barbara started her designs, she took Holy Orders and became Sister Mary Barbara. In her convent, late at night, she continued with her drawings and designs until 150 scenes later it got too much for her. In the 1970s, collectors started buying pieces signed by the artist, and marked 'potted', which indicates a pre-1939 date; in other words, the original rarer pieces. All sorts of Bunnykins Collectables, including figures, have been produced since the 1970s. Take the Bunnykins figure DB29. Produced as a limited edition in the 1980s, and known as 'the Boston Colorway' or 'Touch-down', it has, in the past, made more than £1,000.

In 1996, the Antiques Collectors Club published Louise Irvine's *Bunnykins Collectors Book*. The publication of a book has an interesting effect on a collectable. On the one hand, the book points out what's good, rare and indifferent, so, if you handle enough of the stuff, you could shortly become the leading Bunnykins expert. The problem is that other people will also read the book. But not everyone – and if you are lucky enough to see the £200 Bunnykins teapot being unwrapped at a car boot, you may find the stallholder very happy to take £10 and it's your lucky day! The book also takes the subject to a wider audience and inevitably prices rise steeply as the market suddenly matures. If you have been scouring markets, picking up odd pieces, you could have, say, 50 in your collection, which might have cost you on average £3 each. Total outlay, £150. After the book is published, everyone wants a piece of the action and the average price of your collection is suddenly £80 apiece! Perfectly

possible. You could cash the lot in and pick up £4,000! And, joy of joys, entirely tax free. [4]

The list of moneymaking, collectable ceramics is endless. In a recent Bonhams sale in London, the Beswick Archive Collection was sold, including a rare Beswick model of a pit pony, Spirit of Whitfield, designed by Graham Tongue in 1987. Only four were produced and one made £2,750 at auction in 1994. At the same auction, two wealthy farmers took the bidding to £11,353 for the pit pony, smashing the £3,500 previous Beswick world record price. Every time an astounding price is achieved, the market inevitably reappraises the extant pieces, reinforcing confidence in the collectable. [5]

Why not try vintage radios? Style is all important here. I particularly like the 1931 Pye MM set, with the 'Rising Sun' Art Deco fretted ply cabinet and speaker front. [6] Examples like the Pye MM can be bought restored for between £150 and £200. Will these things appreciate? A school of thought believes that the crude basic valve sets are slices of domestic history that have become increasingly interesting when compared with whizz-bang modern audio equipment.

In 1988, I catalogued with Hilary Kay the first sale at Sotheby's of over 1,920 lots from Elton John's Windsor house. The sale took four days and

Pye MM 1931 'Rising Sun' Radio set

Allen Jones 'Green Table', Elton John sale at Sotheby's, September 1988

appeared in a four-volume, boxed set catalogue. I pulled together volume four, which became known as Phantasmagoria – all the weird and wacky objects that didn't fit any of the other categories. One of the objects which I was particularly sneery about was a Pop Art table, by Allen Jones. The original 1969 version was an uncompromising fetish object showing a life-size female model stark naked apart from her leather boots, gloves and bodice on a mirrored base. The table shown in the illustration is slightly later, made in 1972, in an edition of six, where Mr Jones has toned the thing down a bit by removing the mirror and has put her in some underwear. This one sold at Christie's South Kensington in July 2003 for £32,000. Just think – I could perhaps have bought Sir Elton John's in 1988, for between £5,000 to £7,000.

BARBIE VS BRATZ?

The Barbie scandal in the late 1990s, when Mattel produced ever more dolls, and the bottom dropped out of the market, caused a shudder throughout the doll collectable arena, threatening Barbie's 44-year tenure as queen of the global toy cupboard. Nowadays the makers appear more responsible with genuinely limited editions, called Collector Editions.

The new hip Bratz dolls are the 21st-century hot doll phenomenon and the smart money is that these will surpass Barbie and Sindy as dolly collectables. 150 million of these pouty teen trendies have been sold in only 30 months, appealing to fashion conscious and precocious seven-year-olds. [7]

Another collectable with IPP (International

A group of Barbie dolls

Pulling Power) is Swatch watches. In the mid 1970s, Japanese competition was ruining the ordinary watch market in Switzerland. The SMH (Swiss Corporation for Micro-electronics and Watch-making Industries) was set up and the result was the 1983 launch of the Swatch watch. This spearheaded Europe's watch-making offensive, offering an affordable, stylish, top quality, modern product. Once again, no one could have foreseen another enormous collectable market opening up.

200 million watches later, it is available in a multitude of guises, including Swatch Chrono, Irony, Solar, Musical, The Beep and Access (where the watch doubles up as a ski lift pass!). All Swatch watches are well documented, available in large quantities worldwide, and are cheap to post and store. The ideal money-making collectable! [8]

The Outlaw, 1943; Howard Hughes/Jane Russell, film poster. US Six-sheet, 81 x 81 in, sold at Christie's South Kensington in March 2003 for £52,875

An automatic 'platinum' Swatch watch, signed, no. 12754, with a blue crocodile strap. Sold for €1,434.

RARITY, VALUE AND AUTHENTICITY

If an object is known to be rare, then it is likely to become desirable. But it is vital to ascertain that it really is rare and is not being reproduced or faked.

A recent classic example was the 'unique' film poster, featuring Jane Russell in Howard Hughes' 1943 film, *The Outlaw*, which the censors would not allow to be released. Only two known examples of the poster existed, both owned by the same person. Just before the Christie's South Kensington sale in March 2003, it was announced that one of the two copies had been destroyed, making the survivor unique. This upset a lot of movie poster collectors, but the bidding soared to £52,875!

HOW TO SELL

So, you have made a collection, found some amazing bargains and, suddenly, you lust for cash. How do you go about selling up?

Traditional Auction in London or the Provinces?

You have to weigh up several factors before handing over your collection to an auction house. If the collection is at all specialist, you may well need to shop around. It is possible that XYZ auction house has a wonderful expert in Japanese sword fittings but the painting by John Atkinson Grimshaw should be sold by the ABC auction house because their Victorian Paintings Department is better. [9] So, if you are new to selling antiques, or you have inherited some things and are unsure what to do, or you have been out of the game for a while, then consider consulting a fine art and antiques agent, who is an independent advisor and will tell you the best route to take.

Cost

Cost is crucial when you are making your auction choices. Some auctioneers charge as much as 25 per cent to the vendor and a buyer's premium to each purchaser, which can be as much as 20 per cent. This means you can be losing as much as 45 per cent of the value of your goods in commissions alone. Then there is VAT on the commissions, taking the actual charge in this example, including VAT, to 52.8 per cent.

Not all auction houses charge vendors 25 per cent, but the buyer's premium never changes. At auction, you can get stuck with insurance, at another 1–2 per cent plus VAT, and extras, like illustrations in printed catalogues. Some of the

London rooms will charge £500 per whole colour page, plus VAT. And if you can't deliver to the auction house, you will be charged if the auctioneer doesn't offer free pick up.

So be very certain where you stand with these charges before you sell at auction. Everything is negotiable these days and a fine art and antiques agent will do the grubby negotiation and maybe get you a better deal. [10]

Selling Directly to a Dealer

People shy away from dealers because auction houses have promoted themselves so well, but actually, when selling to a dealer, all you have to do is be careful, as the normal rules of commerce apply.

The dealer is going to try to buy from you as cheaply as possible, so find out the market value of what you are selling first. A dealer belonging to a reputable trade association will pay a decent price for 'fresh to the market, privately sourced goods'. Although you don't get the froth and excitement of an auction, the price from the dealer (in the hand) may be not so bad when compared to the possible price at auction (in the bush). And there will be no commissions or charges being knocked off. [11]

Selling Privately

Increasingly, private owners sell off their possessions at car boots and smaller antiques fairs. Fine, but you must know the value of what you are selling and be thick skinned enough to take the knocks. Be prepared to be jostled, roundly abused, even intimidated by folk trying to beat you down on your asking price. I take exception to some *Bargain Hunt* experts, who endlessly advise the team to 'get the price beaten down'. It is nice if the dealer offers a reduction, but don't expect this as a divine right! [11]

Selling on the Internet

The internet has been a rollercoaster as an auction tool. Sotheby's adopted an internet auction model, which cost the firm around US$50 million and proved a waste of money; their on-line auctions ceased in February 2003.

eBay auctions, however, have been unbelievably successful. Founded by Pierre Omidyar and his wife in September 1995 as a route for collectors to source and trade their collectables inexpensively, it has remained loyal to that ideal. Cheap to use, it turns over US$18 billion a year overall, with collectables, including antiques, accounting for a massive US$1.1 billion each year, with over 85 million worldwide users. The joy is its simplicity. Anyone can log on to and search through eBay. If you want to bid for something you need to register. This only takes a few minutes and allows you to bid and provides you with space, your home page if you so wish, where you can save and watch interesting items.

Buying on eBay

When you are ready to bid, the rules are much the same as a real auction house. Enter your bid and watch the action unfold as the auction comes to a close. If you are successful, there is no additional commission to pay, although you will normally be expected to cover the postage and packing. Just bear in mind: is the description of the goods adequate? Can you clearly see the item in the photographs provided? Has the seller laid out terms and conditions? How much will postage and packing cost? If in any doubt, e-mail the seller and request more information before bidding. You can check the track record of both sellers and buyers in the feedback file. If yours is the winning bid, you get an automatically generated e-mail from eBay.

Selling on eBay

Selling on eBay is almost as easy. Take a few pictures with a digital camera. Have a look at how people sell items similar to yours. Which categories do they use, what are the most successful pictures and which are the best descriptions? Remember, you want to appeal to as many buyers as possible, so your ad needs to stand out.

eBay Quotes and Statistics

In the antiques category on eBay.co.uk, an Oriental item sells every fifteen minutes; a model train sells every two; a map listed in Books & Manuscripts every 25; an item in the 1960s category every 35; an item in the twentieth-century category every eleven; a clock sells every eighteen minutes.

Worried about Fraud?

Collectables as a category experience a small incidence of reported fraud – just one in 10,000.

Categories

From Lilliput Lane Cottages and Star Trek memorabilia to Folk Art and Ethnographica, there are upwards of 15,000 categories, with more being added all the time.

The Cost of eBay

A simple ad in one category with a couple of pictures costs less than a pound. In your advertisement, give the size of the object you are selling (metric and imperial) and, if possible, the weight. Always specify that the buyer pays postage and packaging in addition to his winning bid.

If the item sells, then eBay's selling commission is as follows:

5.25 per cent up to £29.99; 3.25 per cent from £30 – £599.99 and 1.75 per cent from £600.

Once your auction has ended, the earlier roles are reversed. You will contact the buyer, agree on how the item is to be paid for and wait for the money to arrive, having sorted out postage. If your item does not sell, there are no charges apart from the original cost of your ad and you can re-list for free.

eBay Extras

Reserves: Additional Reserve Price Listing Fee. The eBay UK site has recently introduced a reserve listing fee which will be charged at the following rate on all lots listed on the site with a reserve. If the reserve is met and the object sells, then the Additional Reserve Price Listing Fee will be refunded. The reserve fees are:

£0.01p – £49.99: Fee £1

£50.00 – £4,999.99: Fee 2 % of reserve price

£5,000 and up: Fee £100

All reserve fees include VAT.

A word of caution: the old adage, 'time spent in reconnaissance is time well spent', holds good with on-line auctions too, particularly when you are unfamiliar at the beginning. Remember that eBay never ask their users for their user IDs and passwords and any e-mail you may get which purports to come from eBay which asks for personal information, credit card details or eBay passwords is to be treated as bogus. [12]

THE INTERNET AND MONEYMAKING ANTIQUES FOR THE FUTURE

The potential of the internet for collectors has only just begun to be tapped. Lower value collectables have found a secure, inexpensive marketplace via sites such as eBay. For more expensive items, difficult to sell in straight eBay-type online sales, the traditional auction houses, particularly the regional ones, are squaring up to the challenge by producing on-line catalogues so that sales can be viewed worldwide.

Good news for buyers and sellers alike, it will result in a substantial hike in prices. Traditional auctioneers will benefit from the internet, providing they illustrate each lot and can handle the multiple enquiries. The auction house that grips the nettle and reduces commissions and costs on the back of savings afforded by the internet will reap the richest reward of all.

Resources

[1] For information on up-coming Antiques Roadshow events around the country log on to www.bbc.co.uk/antiques

[2] My Little Pony: If you want to know more about collecting these engaging toys then try www.mlptp.com.

[3] To contact Robert Opie and get more information on his amazing collection of packaging, call 020 8997 6419

[4] Try Rosie T's Royal Doulton Bunnykins on www.rosiets.co.uk or
   The Charlton Standard Catalogue of Bunnykins, Jean Dale & Louise Irvine, 1999
   The Bunnykins & Beatrix Potter Price Guide: Royal Doulton, Beswick, Royal Albert, Pinchin and Francis Salmon, Joseph Francis, 1998

[5] *Beswick Pottery – The Charlton Standard Catalogue*, Diane & John Callow, 2000
   The Beswick Price Guide: Price and Colour Guide to Beswick Pottery Collectables, Harvey May, 2001

[6] British Vintage Wireless Society www.bvws.org.uk
   Dates of swap meets at the NEC, 01392 411565.
   A useful website is www.vintageradio.co.uk which takes you on a virtual museum tour.

[7] For collecting Barbie & Bratz dolls go to collectdolls.about.com or www.dollshouse.com or www.rubylane.com or www.dollcloset.com

[8] *Swatch: A Guide for Connoisseurs and Collectors*, Frank Edwards, Firefly Press, 1998

[9] **Auction houses**
   Bonhams, London (020 7393 3900) and with nine salerooms throughout the UK www.bonhams.com
   Christie's (020 7389 2886) www.christies.com
   Sotheby's (020 7293 5000)
   At Sotheby's, for example, you can view and browse catalogues by going to www.sothebys.com – look for the sale of your choice and click 'Browse catalogue'.
   The Society of Fine Art Auctioneers (SOFAA) 01483 225891 www.sofaa.org
   They will provide details of a lot of good firms out of London.
   Dreweatt Neate, until very recently known as **The Fine Art Group** 0870 333 0336 www.thefineartgroup.com
   They have a growing chain of regional auction houses
   For coins and medals try the excellent specialist auctioneers
   Morton and Eden (020 7493 5344). Visit www.mortonandeden.co.uk for upcoming sales

Other regional auctioneers

Halls, Shrewsbury : www.halls-auctioneers.ltd.uk
Lyon & Turnbull, Scotland: www.lyonandturnbull.com
Tennants, Yorkshire: www.tennants.co.uk
Frank R Marshall, Cheshire: www.frankmarshall.co.uk

Goldings, Lincolnshire: www.goldings.co.uk
Bearnes, West Country: www.bearnes.co.uk
Rupert Toovey, Sussex: www.rupert-toovey.com
Gorringes, South East: www.gorringes.co.uk
Brightwells, Herefordshire: www.brightwells.com
Duke's, Dorchester: www.dukes-auctions.com
Wintertons Fine Arts, Staffordshire & Derbyshire: www.winterton.com
Gildings, Market Harborough: www.gildings.com
Lawrences, Crewkerne www.lawrences.co.uk
Bigwoods, Stratford upon Avon: www.bigwoodauctioneers.co.uk
Richard Winterton, Burton on Trent:
Email: adrianrathbone@btconnect.com
Auction catalogues can be viewed on line through specialist sites such as:
www.invaluable.com
www.icollector.com
www.ukauctioneers.com

[10] **Fine Art Agents**
   Robert Holden London W1 T: 020 7437 6010
   robertholden@btinternet.com
   Jeremy Rye & Associates Welshpool, Powys T: 01686 640802
   Tim Sammons London W1 T: 020 7629 1386
   artagents@timothy-sammons.co.uk
   Stancliffe & Glover London W1 T: 020 7468 7454
   Webb Valuations Fine Art Ltd 49 Berkeley Square, London W1J 5AZ
   T: 020 7491 3941 davidwebb@webbvaluations.com
   Tim Wonnacott & Associates PO Box 536, East Grinstead
   RH19 4XH T: 01342 811757 tw@timwonnacott.com

[11] **Dealers**
   LAPADA (The Association of Art & Antiques Dealers)
   T: 020 7823 3511 www.lapada.co.uk
   BADA (The British Antique Dealers' Association)
   T: 020 7589 4128 www.bada.org

[11] **Antiques fairs and car boot sales:**
   I recommend that you subscribe to:
   the **Antiques Trade Gazette**, a good source for salerooms, fairs and general interest. Credit card hotline: 020 7420 6601
   www.antiquestradegazette.com
   Collect It! A glossy and very informative magazine with masses of news about collectables. Subscription Line 01206 851117

[12] See eBay explained on www.eBay.co.uk's homepage: a good tool for navigating the site and learning how to buy and sell successfully. For checking up on feedback on eBay buyers and sellers, try http://pages.ebay.co.uk/services/forum/feedback.html.

2

PAUL ATTERBURY ON
TRAVEL

TIM WONNACOTT

' Well-versed in the traditions and myths of the Victorian age, Paul is equally happy talking about pottery and porcelain, designers and architects, steam trains and ships – a true polymath. You sense these wide-ranging interests in the way he has addressed the collecting elements in this chapter. '

By 1900, travellers benefited directly from the achievements of Victorian entrepreneurs and engineers. It was possible to cross the Atlantic on a large modern steamship in comfort in under seven days, travel on a train at high speed, and explore by rail much of Europe, Russia, Asia, the Far East and the Americas, ride round cities in electric tramcars, and be carried in safety beneath those same city streets on subway systems.

SEA

Between the 1890s and 1914, the modern superliner was born, a fast and well-appointed vessel capable of carrying hundreds of passengers in luxury. Every industrialised country tried to outdo its rivals in the size, comfort and speed of its ships, then still the backbone of global trade. Shipping lines became household names – Hamburg Amerika, Cunard, White Star, French Line, P&O. Equally famous were the ships – *Mauretania*, *Aquitania*, *France*, *Kaiser Wilhelm*, *Olympic* and, inevitably, the ill-fated *Titanic*.

With their lavish interiors, these ships established new standards of excellence. Their styling was imaginative and historical in inspiration, echoing the seventeenth and eighteenth centuries and styling associated with great hotels. A specific maritime style had yet to emerge.

A ship poster for the Queen Mary, sold at Christie's South Kensington for £667 in 1998

Ship's bell from HMS Conqueror, sold at Sotheby's for £450 in 1995

Many great ships remained in service through the 1920s, regularly refitted to modern standards, but still in traditional styles. Only in the 1930s was the truly modern ocean liner created, with interiors by noted contemporary designers. The pioneer was the French Line's *Ile de France*, but the look soon spread to Italian and German ships, and ultimately to those great rivals of the North Atlantic route, Cunard's *Queen Mary* and French Line's *Normandie*, ships that defined the Art Deco style.

Maritime modernism was carried on through the 1950s and 1960s, culminating in the magnificent *QE2*, the last of a long and glorious line of ships built primarily for transatlantic service. When the *QM2* came into service early in 2004, there were echoes of the famous old *Queen Mary*. The new ship was promoted as the largest, most exciting and most luxurious ship ever – but certainly not the fastest! Time will tell whether she matches the reputation still enjoyed by her namesake, nearly forty years after coming out of service.

In the end, all ships go to the breaker's yard. Despite this, many things survive for the collector. Such collecting is international and well established, but maritime memorabilia, as with railway and aviation memorabilia, have no intrinsic value. It is driven by the chance survival of objects designed either for a short shelf life, or to be thrown away. However, the combination of chance survival and nostalgia is a powerful cocktail.

The most popular area is promotional material. Coloured posters, promoting shipping lines and particular ships, were produced regularly from the 1890s, but the golden age for collectors was from the 1920s to the 1950s. The appeal and value of shipping posters are influenced by the standing of the company, the status of the ship, the artist involved, and the image's graphic quality. Top of the tree, and worth £6,000 to £8,000 or more, will be posters by French artist Cassandre. Near the bottom, worth a couple of hundred, will be a poster advertising a minor shipping line or ship, designed either anonymously or by an artist with little collector appeal. In between is a huge choice, depending on budget. Far more available, and more accessible in cost terms, are brochures and other publicity material, including postcards. Showing ships and interiors, these range in price from a couple of pounds to about £30.

There's also liner ephemera, including anything from or directly associated with a ship. When ships are broken up, their fixtures and fittings are sometimes sold, so furniture, crockery and cutlery, along with equipment, signage and bells, can be found. Ideally, all items should carry the ship's name or the shipping line's badge. Also available are menus, luggage labels, cabin stationery and other printed ephemera. Value is again determined by the ship's status, with a menu from the *Queen Mary* being far more desirable than one from a cross-Channel ferry. Much is available under £50. The exception is the *Titanic*, with memorabilia directly associated with the ship fetching thousands of pounds on the international market.

RAIL

The majority of the world's major railway networks had been built by 1900. Pioneering work by Pullman, among others, launched international rail travel, with high standards of comfort being maintained regardless of national or state boundaries.

In the early twentieth century, famous names such as the *Orient Express* emerged. This pattern was maintained after the First World War, and the networks of both international and domestic luxury trains were steadily expanded, with trains such as *Le Train Bleu* and the *Golden Arrow* becoming household names. Named luxury trains were soon found in the timetables of every country with developed railway networks, including North and South America, Russia, China, Japan, Australia and Africa.

As with ships, promotion was dependent upon colourful, well-designed posters and publicity brochures, many using striking avant garde imagery by leading artists and designers. House styling and branding were employed to promote their routes by many railway companies, such as the big four (GWR, LNER, LMS and SR), which emerged in Britain from 1923. The most important collecting legacy of this period is the railway poster, with a huge diversity of style and subject, promoting not just trains, but the journey and the destination as well. Railway companies pioneered modern tourism, helping create holiday destinations such as the Alps, the French Riviera, coastal resorts in Cornwall, Devon and Yorkshire, and whole regions, such as Wales and Scotland.

Railway posters range from under £100 to up to £10,000. In Britain, posters designed for the LNER by Tom Purvis usually fetch between £1,000 and

THE PASS OF ABERGLASLYN

by Norman Wilkinson

NORTH WALES

BRITISH RAILWAYS

A rail poster of North Wales from 1930 by Norman Wilkinson for British Railways. Sold at Christie's South Kensington for £470 in 2003

and there are several dedicated auction houses in Britain. A typical catalogue includes documents, books, railway stationery, labels and notices, crockery and cutlery, uniforms and equipment, lamps and clocks, signalling paraphernalia, station seats, framed pictures and advertisements.

Primary interest is reserved for cast iron and enamel lineside and station notices, station name boards and bits of locomotives. Sought after are enamel station names, in the standard totem style introduced by British Railways from 1948. Recent sales of enamel totems include Stamford Town (BR Eastern Region) for £6,700; Bath Green Park (BR Western Region) for £4,600; and Darlington (BR NE Region) for £4,400. These are high prices because of rarity. Plenty still sell for under £500. Prices are affected by region (GWR is always popular, SR less so) and by rarity of station (closed or open, size of station and thus number of totems issued and number surviving).

Collectors fight over cast numbers, maker's plates, whistles, shed plates and gauges and controls, but provenance is all. However, Mecca is represented by a locomotive's cast metal nameplate. When the locomotives made by GWR, LNER, LMS or SR were broken up in the 1960s, the nameplates were available for a few pounds. Now they fetch thousands. Again, provenance is all, and the plates have to have good documentation. The current nameplate auction record is £54,000 for *Gresley P2 Cock o'the North*, with the same price being paid recently for *LMS Coronation* and *Sir William Stanier*. Some are more popular than others; a nameplate from a Gresley Class A4 Pacific of LNER would probably fetch over £55,000, while one from some humble or anonymous industrial tank engine will be a few hundreds.

£8,000 (classic images fetching the most), but many by other important designers are still available for under £1,000. For the collector of more modest means, widely available are publicity brochures, luggage labels, tickets, postcards and other similar examples of ephemera.

Unlike ships, some classic era trains still survive, so it is still possible to experience, if only as a spectator, the glory of the steam engine, and the splendour of Pullman travel. This has generated interest in all aspects of railwayana,

Concorde Nose Cone, sold at Christie's Paris for €470,250 in 2003

Zeppelin Reederei, sold for £2,760. A very rare porcelain wall plaque depicting LZ127 Graf Zeppelin over the Bodensee, decorated in blue with gilt border, by Heinrich and Co, Bavaria, sold for £1,092.50. Both sold at Christie's South Kensington in 1999

Nameplates from major classes of diesels are following this route, and interest is increasing in name and number plates from non-British locomotives.

AIR

Orville and Wilbur Wright's flier first staggered into the air in 1903. From this primitive beginning, aeroplanes and air travel quickly developed. By the early 1920s, an aeroplane had crossed the Atlantic and the first scheduled passenger services were operating. Through the 1920s and 1930s, many global air routes were pioneered, but airliners were slow, noisy, small and not particularly safe. Few could take as many as 30 passengers and, while passengers were carried in style, tickets were expensive. So, until the 1950s, most people travelled by train, ship or bus. In the late 1930s, range and safety and comfort standards were greatly improved by a new generation of large flying boats, and by airships, which, briefly, seemed to represent the future. However, everything was changed by the Second World War and, so, in the 1950s, modern air travel was born. By the 1960s, the jet airliner was dominant.

The collecting of aeroplane memorabilia does not enjoy the same international popularity as rail and maritime memorabilia, partly because there is less to collect and less nostalgia appeal. Again, interest focuses on the 1920s to 1950s, with enthusiasm for dynamic and avant garde posters and publicity material. However, the market is smaller and prices lower.

Also of interest are manufacturers' brochures promoting particular aircraft, photographs, cabin ephemera, postcards and badged items. Crockery or other items carrying the speedbird logo of Imperial Airways are always popular, particularly if associated with the Empire flying boats of the late 1930s and 1940s. Point of sale material, particularly aircraft models from the windows of travel agencies, can fetch £200 to £1,000, depending on size, type of aircraft and airline. Dating by livery change is important – short-lived liveries or airlines can attract higher prices.

The market for bits of aeroplanes is also limited. Early propellers and gauges attract buyers, but everything else tends to be too technical. The exception is the airship. Airships enjoyed a chequered history during the 1930s due to spectacular disasters, culminating in the destruction of the *Hindenburg*. Somewhat perversely, collectors enjoy disasters, and so airship memorabilia tend to fetch more than anything to do with aircraft. The field includes bits of airships, preferably from famous examples, documents, cabin ephemera and publicity material.

An aircraft that may change the pattern is *Concorde*. No other airliner in the history of civil aviation has provoked so emotional a public response. Now the aircraft is history, the market for *Concorde* memorabilia is beginning to grow, and may represent an area for future expansion. Items with the greatest appeal are those with the best provenance.

SPACE

When the long-held fantasy of space travel became real in the 1950s, with the first successful artificial satellites, a different type of space enthusiasm began to emerge, encouraged by manned space exploration by Russia and the United States. However, reality never diminished fantasy and the co-existence of the two explains the enduring popularity of space fiction in the cinema and on television – and the cult status of *Doctor Who*, *Thunderbirds*, *Star Trek* and *Star Wars*. Choice is restricted for the collector of real space ephemera. Most popular, and most accessible, are signed astronaut photographs: American and Russian heroes of the 1960s and early 1970s space programmes are most desirable. Much harder to collect are relics of space exploration, such as space suits, module equipment, instruments, and bits of rockets and other space vehicles. The field is so small it only has highly specialised collector appeal.

Signed photo by NASA Apollo 1 astronauts. Sold at Christie's New York for US$12,650

Resources

Further reading

Collector's Guide to Railwayana, Handel Kardas,
    Ian Allen Books, 2001
Also specialist railway magazines often feature
ephemera. There are books on maritime
memorabilia and shipping postcards, but no one
title covers the whole field. Aviation is similarly
scattered in reading terms, as are travel posters.

Further information

Many major auction houses hold regular sales of
travel posters and ship and aviation memorabilia.
For railwayana, there are specialised auction
houses, including Sheffield Railwayana Auctions,
Onslows, Solent Railwayana Auctions and many
others, some of which specialise even further; for
example, on tickets or luggage labels. Postcard
fairs are a useful source, as most postcard dealers
sell railway, ship and aviation cards.

TIMELINE

Locomotive nameplate collecting is a phenomenon of the post-
steam era in Britain; that is, after 1968. Initially collected by
serious enthusiasts, nameplates were both relatively common
and very cheap. The last 20 years have seen major changes, with
prices for plates from top classes of steam locomotives rising
rapidly. Prices are increased if the cabside or smokebox number
plate accompanies the nameplate. Prices of plates from diesel
locomotives are now rising fast.

The nameplate and cabside number plate 7014 from
Caerhays Castle, a Great Western Castle Class locomotive,
would have cost £15–£20 in 1968, £1,000 by 1980, ten times
that by 1990, and made £30,400 in 2003. This price rise may
not be sustained into the future with the emergence of a
generation of collectors who have no direct personal memories
of steam locomotives (other than preserved examples).

British Railways 1940 nameplate and number plate, sold for £30,400
at Sheffield Railwayana Auctions in 2003

CRYSTAL BALL

Prices for travel material are always affected
by perceptions of quality and rarity. Collectors
should aim high, but not be affected by
temporary fashions. In the railway area, some
things are still cheap – good original
photographs, particularly from the nineteenth
century, luggage labels and other paperwork
(some a hundred years old and from obscure
railway companies) are still available for 50p.
Ship and airline memorabilia will probably rise,
particularly at the lower ends of the market. A
menu from the Queen Mary can still be found
for about £15, and that is cheap. As in every
field, condition is paramount.

Two menu cards and concert programmes from RMS Carpathia, 1912

3

MARC ALLUM ON
COMMUNICATIONS:
TELEGRAPHY, RADIO, TV, TELEPHONES, NEWSPAPERS AND POST

TIM WONNACOTT

It's a joy to sit next to Marc on the miscellaneous table at an *Antiques Roadshow*. If something really tricky turns up, here is a man who knows about everything from toys and games to South American art from the pre-Columbian period, via rock and pop, 1960s fashion and Eskimo carvings. A director of a busy London auctioneers, Marc has youth and boundless enthusiasm.

Whether you're 20, 40 or even 60 years old, some medium for transferring information or communicating with your fellow human beings will have shaped your life. Think of an event like the death of John F. Kennedy in 1963. How did you hear of his assassination? By newspaper, television newsflash or radio? Over the decades, the power of such media has increased, passing information at ever greater speeds to more people, in more innovative ways. Do we take them for granted? The answer is probably yes, but I still remember my parents having the first colour television in our street in 1970. My office drawer houses a museum of mobile telephones, all smaller and more complicated than the last, and all in just ten years. The technology, the tangible objects of those applications, and the events, are all irrevocably entwined in a melee of scientific advance, design, macabre interest and collectability. So where do we begin?

TELEGRAPHY

When Guglielmo Marconi set sail for England in 1896, his wireless telegraphy system was sufficiently improved to demonstrate it to the General Post Office. Although Marconi did not invent wireless telegraphy, he is credited with producing the first practical and commercially viable system.

In 1908, Marconi had no choice but to take over as managing director to save his ailing company, having previously been in a development role. The Dalston factory had to be closed after just three years and the transatlantic message service was still unprofitable. The positive news coverage needed to demonstrate the benefits of wireless telegraphy came in the form of a marine accident in 1909, when a White Star vessel, the SS *Republic,* collided with an Italian vessel, the SS *Florida*. The *Republic* was badly damaged and the radio cabin was crushed, but the Marconi operator, Jack Binns, was able to repair the Marconi apparatus. His contact with the shore station, some 42 kilometres away at Sianconset, meant that other ships in the vicinity were able to save over 1,700 people, despite the *Republic*'s loss. Marconi personally presented Binns with a gold watch.

In 1910, after brutally murdering his wife, Dr Crippen fled across the Atlantic on the SS *Montrose,* pursued by Inspector Dew of Scotland Yard. Although Crippen had a head start, Dew was on the faster *Laurentic*, intending to overtake and arrest Crippen on his arrival in Canada. The whole process was fuelled by wireless, and while Captain Kendall of the *Montrose* ensured Crippen remained oblivious of his fate, wireless telegraphy kept the press updated and caused a media frenzy. Even Crippen was heard to remark to Captain Kendall, 'what a wonderful invention wireless is'. This 'first' ensures that articles associated with Crippen are still very collectable: his signature starts at about £100. In 1999, a photograph album was brought into an *Antiques Roadshow* in Torquay, compiled by a Mr Belcher, an important Scotland Yard figure in the early 1900s. The album contained photographs of Crippen, amongst others, and was valued at £5,000 to £10,000.

The tragedy of the *Titanic*, on 15 April 1912, has gained almost mythical status, and any item associated with it makes huge sums. In 1992, a collection of original signals sent between the *Titanic* and other ships in the vicinity, including the *Carpathia,* was put to auction. This set of 85 Marconi telegraph messages sold for £66,000. The discovery of the wreck in 1985 further hyped interest, as did the ensuing film, exhibitions and Imax productions; consequently, the signals could well be worth two to three times that today.

An early Marconi coherer receiver with patent marks for 1895 and 1906 sold at auction in 2000 for £35,000, against an estimate of £2,000 to £3,000, and an early Marconi magnetic detector from 1910 sold for £10,350. These prices illustrate the importance of such early equipment.

RADIO

Great disasters attract the most attention and airwaves carry the bad news. However, the airwaves have another use, too – entertainment! In 1922 Marconi started broadcasting a weekly programme of calibration signals for the growing number of wireless amateurs. By September 1923 the first public wireless exhibition was opened at the Central Hall in Westminster. There were over

The classic Ecko AD65 designed by the architect Wells Coates, £400–£20,000 at auction, depending on colour

40 exhibitors, and models such as the Marconiphone 'Crystal A' Type RB3 M2 would have been on show, costing a whopping nine pounds ten shillings, including earphones. Current price for this early set would be £250 to £350 at auction.

Some collectors concentrate on the cheaper alternative, crystal sets, a much simpler apparatus, needing no batteries. They use a mineral crystal such as galena, which is literally tickled by a tiny wire called a 'cat's whisker'. Finding a spot on the crystal that produced a good enough signal for the headphones could be longwinded and frustrating. Most sets were made for short range reception using local medium wave stations and could only cope with a maximum of two headphone sets. The most collectable sets tend to be the novelty examples such as the 1924 'Uncle Tom' set made by the Grafton China Works of A. B. Jones & Co. Designed by J. P. Gowland, it takes the form of a squat man in a stove pipe hat. Current value is between £500 and £700. The original purchase price was

Product architecture, the TS502 for Brionvega, £200 at auction for an orange example

seventeen shillings and sixpence.

The technology soon spawned more advanced and stylish designs. By 1932, the architect Wells Coates had designed the now classic Ecko AD65 in a superb circular bakelite cabinet, one of the first truly modern consumer items. At eleven pounds eleven shillings, it was not cheap, but the basic brown or black bakelite versions now sell at auction for £400 to £600. If you were wealthy enough to commission a more expensive green cabinet, current value is difficult to predict. An

example reputedly sold in 1993 for £20,000.

Commissioning eminent designers to style an item, be it a lemon squeezer or a chair, has always been industry's answer to placing its product accurately, and, as the AD65 displayed, radios are no exception. The Castiglioni brothers – Livio, Peir Giacomo and Achille – designed in many disciplines from town planning to furniture. The famous Phonola radio of 1939, from the studio of Livio and Peir Giacomo, was the first Italian bakelite-cased radio, and, by all accounts, the only radio to be

Space age design for the masses, the Nivico 3240 helmet television for JVC, £200 at auction

permanently exhibited in New York's Museum of Modern Art. Like the AD65, the case colour is a major factor in determining value: the dark green case is one of the rarest. Expect to pay a few hundred pounds at auction for a standard model.

In 1964, the collaboration between Italian designer Marco Zanuso and the German Richard Sapper saw the TS502 radio produced by Brionvega. Zanuso's experimentation with new materials means that this classic radio is an essential for the modern design connoisseur. Expect to pay around £200 at auction for an orange example.

The term 'Pop Design' originated in the 1950s and came to symbolise the increasing strength of popular culture and the demand for bright colours and wild designs. However, the use of cheaper materials and gimmicky design was the real start of built-in obsolescence, and some of these items are consequently more difficult to find.

TELEVISION

Several million sets were sold prior to the Coronation in 1953, and, as a form of mass communication, the television has since revolutionised our lives. If you can bear to watch in black and white, the Nivico 3240 GM television, made for JVC in about 1970, is a pop classic. Its space age helmet shape epitomises the period and the orange version is far more striking than the white. £200 at auction seems to secure a reasonable example.

TELEPHONES

When Alexander Graham Bell invented the telephone in 1876, I'm sure he was aware of the importance of his discovery. In the last few years, the real cost of making telephone calls has steadily fallen. When I was a boy, calling relatives in Australia was expensive, and only occurred at Christmas. The handsets that we use today are varied and ever cheaper designs constantly flow into the shops. Classic designs, however, will always lure collectors. People still continue to use them, often finding them more aesthetically appealing than their modern counterparts. Take the DHB 1001 bakelite telephone designed by Jean Heiberg, who studied under Henri Mattisse and is well known for his own paintings and sculpture. He designed the DHB in 1930 for L. M. Ericsson, a company already with a reputation for innovation. Made under licence throughout Europe and America, it became the benchmark for telephone

Art meets industry, Jean Heiberg's DHB 1001 bakelite telephone. Originals are rare but later models made under licence start at £30

First generation immobile telephone, the Motorola Transportable Phone, £40 on eBay

design and continued as the standard for telephones until the 1950s. Black is the basic colour and can be purchased very cheaply at auction for £30 to £50. Expect to pay £100 for the rarer ivory, and as much as £350 for the green.

When mobile telephones first arrived, they weren't very mobile. Nicknamed 'brick phones', models such as the Motorola 4500X came with a cumbersome battery and electronics pack. They were also extremely expensive, costing around £1,000 in the 1980s. Their reputation as toys for

wealthy executives has disappeared in a relatively short time, as the miniaturisation of technology has moved in leaps and bounds. It now seems unusual not to have a mobile telephone. With internet, built-in cameras and video conferencing telephones, what now seems gimmicky will very shortly be the norm. Retro chic means that some fashionistas have been using the bricks again. Models such as the 4500X have their place in history but can easily be purchased for £40. On-line auction sites, such as eBay, generally have a few examples.

NEWSPAPERS

More down to earth forms of communication, such as newspapers and the post, still influence us greatly. As an auctioneer, I often find myself in situations where the owner of an old newspaper proudly proclaims the worth of a *Daily Mail* 1953 Coronation edition. The problem is that post-war patriotism meant that millions were kept, so are consequently worth little. Neville Chamberlain's 'peace in our time' headline might be worth a few pounds, but what collectors really like are headlines such as 'Bravo Bleriot', with Bleriot pictured on the front of a 1908 *Daily Graphic*. This will cost £15 to £20. There is also the inevitable attraction to infamous events, such as the R101 airship disaster in October 1930. Forty-six people died in the accident and a *Daily Express* with the tragic headline will cost around £20.

Interesting postal history, airship mail from 1934 delivered in style on a Zeppelin, £80 from a postal history dealer

POST

Postal history is extremely collectable, and, as opposed to stamp collecting, enthusiasts are also interested in the envelope and contents. Covers which commemorate the first mail flights between countries are good examples and, just as disaster spells collectability, the strange world of crash covers appeals to postal history collectors. Mail recovered from a crashed mail plane, or, better still a Zeppelin, can carry large premiums. For example, a 1934 nine penny London to Bakia, Brazil, letter, carried by the Zeppelin *Seiger* 260, will cost around £80.

Resources

Further Reading

Design of the 20th Century, Charlotte & Peter Fiell, Taschen, 1999
Designing the 21st Century, edited by Charlotte & Peter Fiell, Taschen, 2001
Bakelite Radios, Robert Hawes in collaboration with Gad Sassower, Chartwell Books, 1996
The Cat's Whisker: 50 years of Radio Design, Jonathan Hill, Oresko Books, London, 1978
Radio Radio, Jonathan Hill, Sunrise Press, 1986
Miller's Collectables Price Guide, Madeleine Marsh (General Editor), Octopus Publishing Group
Telephones Antique to Modern, Kate E. Dooner, Schiffer Publishing, 1992

Internet Sites

www.marconicalling.com/museum/events
www.titanicmemorabilia.co.uk (British Titanic Society)
www.henry-aldridge.co.uk (Auctioneers specialising in Titanic)
www.sowdendesign.com (All about this design studio)
www.banaldesign.com (George Sowden designs on sale)
www.telephonelines.net (Dealers in all kinds of telephones)

TIMELINE

The fascination with *Titanic* material knows no bounds and any collector willing to speculate in this area will certainly be making an investment. The original group of Titanic Marconi telegraph signals were perhaps worth £100 in 1913, £1,000 in 1950 and sold for £66,000 in 1992. Today, the signals would be likely to sell at auction for between £120,000 and £150,000.

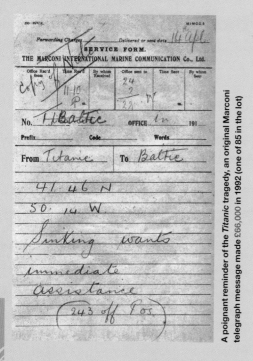

A poignant reminder of the *Titanic* tragedy, an original Marconi telegraph message made £66,000 in 1992 (one of 85 in the lot)

The Miram 100 telephone, designed for Olivetti by the Sowden design studio, might well be a collectable in the future

CRYSTAL BALL

If you are investing for profit, then you often have to take greater financial gambles over a greater period of time, which means that buying rare Marconi items now should pay handsome dividends in the future. Purchasing low value technological pieces may pay in time, as their disposable nature leaves few original consumer items in good condition. My advice is to collect items with good associations, perhaps with an established or up-and-coming designer. Take the Miram 100 telephone for Olivetti by the Sowden design studio. Could the sleek originality of this 1980s design have increased future collectability? Finally, buy only what you can live with and don't be seduced into liking an object just because it is potentially valuable!

4

LARS THARP ON
CELEBRITY AND NOTORIETY

TIM WONNACOTT

"I have known Lars for over 25 years. We have shared podiums, rostrums, studios and dressing rooms, a memorable television shower scene, even transatlantic liners! I never ceased to be amazed by his intellect and by his sense of humour. Only he could contemplate the impossibly broad topic of twentieth-century celebrity as a collecting area and weave such a prescient chapter."

The twentieth century was one of unparalleled speed – of travel, communication, creation, destruction and resurrection, popularity and revulsion. As the tempo quickened, and people became wealthier in the west, fashions rose and fell, were revived, reviled and revisited. The 'celebrity' has played an ever more prominent role, each decade washing up endless lists of them, each ousting the last. As Andy Warhol predicted in the 1960s, 'everyone will be famous for fifteen minutes'. Interest in personality really intensified after the First World War, with the widening of popular culture, made possible by new technology boosted by war.

In the early 1900s, the tobacco industry sought to build brand loyalty: a printed picture card was inserted in every cigarette packet to encourage smokers to up the habit. Playing on 'completism', the human need to acquire a complete set, the cigarette card was a brilliant wheeze, and was followed by the tea and coffee industry, as well as comics, magazines and children's sweets.

Cigarette card subjects included transport, leading world figures, and sports. Today, few of great-grandpa's cigarette card collections fetch serious prices among collectors. But, just occasionally, a forgotten hero is still capable of hitting a good home run. Take 'The Flying

Dutchman', Honus Wagner (1874–1955). A famous baseball player and early anti-smoker, Mr Wagner was angered to discover his image being used without his permission on a cigarette card series issued in 1909. At his insistence, the card was withdrawn. Consequently, the full series of all 150 subjects became impossible to complete. A century later and the price on Honus's head is determined not by his celebrity but by an historical advertising goof making him very rare. Cannily, the manufacturers had hit on a way of boosting the selling power of their brand, as all uninformed collectors would carry on smoking, still on the look-out for the missing man. Moral: celebrity may wither but rarity remains – and ultimately determines price.

Warhol's pop images represent the spirit of the 1970s. However, the Warhol Estate has recently rejected certain 'Warhol' editions, causing turmoil in their market value.

THE FILM INDUSTRY

As the movies got under way, picture houses flourished and stardom grew. After seeing Rudolf Valentino on screen, millions throughout the world felt they knew him personally. Stars such as Gloria Swanson, Charlie Chaplin, Fred Astaire, Douglas Fairbanks, Greta Garbo, Laurence Olivier, Vivien Leigh, Judy Garland, Clark Gable, Bette Davis and Humphrey Bogart were cast in films, guaranteeing millions at the box office. Swooning at the movies was common and continued on stage half a century later with Elvis and The Beatles.

The star business meant star accessories. Programmes, periodicals, posters, signed autographs (many not actually signed at all, but printed with a facsimile signature) were bought in their millions. Songs and numbers promoting the new musicals were recorded on newly invented shellac (later vinyl).

Even from the talkies era, only the brightest stars still flicker today. But prices have continued climbing for the posters advertising cult movies, often brilliant graphics in their own right. Strongest sellers feature the biggest names; for example, £25,000 for the 1933 poster of the classic *King Kong*. This depicts Fay Wray in the grip of the giant ape, which is savaging a biplane while perched on top of another (inanimate) celebrity, the Empire State Building.

Sex sells – and sex/screen goddess Marilyn Monroe is one of the most famous of all post Second World War movie stars. Prices for posters of her films, such as *Gentlemen Prefer Blondes* (1953) and *Some Like It Hot* (1959), and for her personal effects rise well beyond prices for second-rank stars. Her signature alone makes between £500 and £1,000; a signed photograph, £3,000 to

£5,000; her blouse from *Bus Stop* (1956) £5,500; and a pair of her sunglasses was sold in 1996 for £2,530. In any market where otherwise ordinary objects can fetch inflated sums if they have belonged to a star, it becomes essential to prove the connection with the original owner: provenance is all.

But, in addition to her looks, screen presence and colourful private life, one other very important factor took Marilyn Monroe from mere celebrity to icon status: death.

DEATH AND NOTORIETY

Death has always drawn the masses. In the eighteenth century, crowds lined London's Oxford Street as the condemned 'went west' from Newgate to Tyburn Tree (today's Marble Arch). In the west, we no longer experience death on the almost daily basis as our great-grandparents did. Mortality is now so invisible that it has become taboo. When death pricks our bubble, we simply have to look – and, combined with sex, royalty or power, it becomes even more fascinating.

Monroe's immortality was clinched by her involvement with another icon. America's most charismatic president, John F. Kennedy, with his glamorous wife and family, was the republic's equivalent to royalty: young and attractive; a speaker with vision; the most powerful man in the world. Suffering from a bad back, the president took pain relief in a rocking chair in his White House office. Today several internet sites are offering a modern chair based on the Kennedy model for prices ranging from US$210 to £297. In the 1996 Sotheby sale of effects from the estate of the late John F. Kennedy, the original rocker

President Kennedy's rocking chair. Sold at Sotheby's New York in April 1996 for $442,500

fetched a spectacular US$442,500 – almost two thousand times its value as an ordinary chair.

Diana, Princess of Wales, was another figure upon whom these factors of light and shade also flickered. Shortly before her premature death (some say courted by the very lifestyle she adopted) a collection of her gowns realised nearly US$5 million at a 1997 Christie's sale. With the written contents of Diana's letters still under her estate's copyright protection, it will be several years before the texts are likely to be commercially available. Just occasionally, however, out pops a

The Cartier original fetched just under £498,000 at the Sotheby's 'Windsor Jewels' sale in Geneva, 1987. This modern replica, also in rubies, sapphires and diamonds, was made shortly after the 1987 Windsor sale and retailed for around one tenth of the price of the celebrated original.

minor scrap: such as the Valentine's card addressed to 'Sgt Lewis from Diana' and inscribed 'Not many men will receive a Valentine's card from Princess Diana . . . and you're one of them!!!' Estimated pre-sale at £200 to £300, the card made £2,000 in 2003. Yet, since her death, hardly a day goes by without her image appearing in a national paper. The resourceful, money-driven media, self-appointed guardians of Diana's flame, feed on the very scandals they condemn. In a hundred years, that flame may burn no brighter than that of an earlier would-have-been Queen, Caroline of Brunswick, spurned wife of George IV. For now, however, collectors still dig deep.

Although it is nearly 70 years since the abdication of Edward VIII, his marriage to America divorcee Wallis Simpson has generated shelves of books and reels of television and film. In 1987, when Sotheby's sold the jewels exchanged between Edward and Wallis, universal interest in their unique story brought frenzied bidding from the Americas to Japan. Yet again, provenance took prices through the roof, totalling over US$40 million.

DISASTERS AND WAR

Had the bejewelled passengers aboard a particular ocean liner safely disembarked in New York, with reminiscences of a wonderful maiden voyage – and maybe a slight *frisson* as they recalled icebergs on the horizon – the whole *Titanic* memorabilia industry would never have been. Eighty years after her tragic sinking, it continues to grow, although, in terms of suffering and human lives lost, there have been far more catastrophic ocean disasters. Some explain the relentless rise of the *Titanic* phenomenon as a threnody for the decade, a way of mourning both the millions lost in battle and the passing of an epoch.

The phenomenon gathers pace. The binoculars which never reached the fated bridge fetch tens of thousands of pounds, and other relics – a steward's watch, frozen at the time he jumped into the ocean – still come to the surface. But for how long? Is the *Titanic* market unsinkable? And now the wreck has been located, deep-sea robots are scooping up buckets of coal, to be sold in sugar-lump size with certificates of authenticity, at prices ranging from US$20 (for splinters of coal in hollow glass hearts and crucifixes on a chain) to US$120 for a centimetre cube.

The major players in the greatest of all twentieth-century disasters – man-made war – have yet to be taken up with the vigour shown by the followers of the Napoleonic and Crimean wars in the nineteenth century. There are plenty of collectors of figures such as Nelson, Napoleon and Wellington, but one of the few appealing figures of the Second World War – to Brits and Americans alike – is Winston Churchill.

With the end of the Cold War in 1989, its most potent symbol became a souvenir quarry. Within a few days the Berlin Wall, an otherwise unremarkable graffiti-covered breeze-block and cement structure, was reduced to chunks – each with a price, each a trophy charged with memories of a sundered nation. Likewise, East Germany's erstwhile masters, past presidents of the Communist Party, may today be bought at every souvenir shop in the former Soviet Union, transformed with Russian irony into traditional *matryoshka* dolls. Putin contains his predecessors, right back to a minuscule Comrade Lenin. Such witty souvenirs are a must for collectors of political memorabilia – of the twentieth century, or simply of satire.

Competent amateur artists rarely reach high prices at auction . . . unless they're famous.
The Sea from La Capponica by Winston Spencer Churchill, sold at Sotheby's in 2003 for £84,000.

COLLECTORS OF THE CENTURY: THE NEW BUYERS

But who are today's collectors of twentieth-century celebrity and notoriety? By the 1990s, a substantial number of the world's billionaires were young entrepreneurs, technology princes, sportsmen, stars of film and popular music – celebrities, in fact. They aren't looking to recreate their grandfather's past; they're children of the twentieth century, a century in love with itself. Their total spending power, and their influence on the tastes of their contemporaries, is awesome. It is further fuelled by advertising campaigns which associate big celebrity names with big brands. It's just a continuation of the Honus Wagner baseball card, but in a world now teeming with markets and money. As one sociologist has said, 'if it hasn't been seen on television, it hasn't happened'. Whether the 21st century will continue to worship at the dusty altar of twentieth-century celebrity is another question . . .

Celebrity – that fickle fame seen by Andy Warhol for the bubble it is – is merely the hothouse in a larger garden where rarer, and more enduring, plants grow in the shadows. Collectors who hope to make money in the long term should bear this in mind. Once that first wave of nostalgia for some recent person or event has bloomed, it might be rash to wait for a second flowering.

FICTIONAL CELEBRITIES

The most powerful twentieth-century celebrities are not of flesh and blood but of plastic. There's serious money in fictional figures. It started slowly, with *Steamboat Willie* (1928). The young Mr Disney changed Willie's name to Mickey Mouse and manufacturers applied for rights to reproduce his image. Disney toys were made in their millions, at first in tinplate, then in plastic. The 1929 Tipp & Co tinplate Mickey motorbike group, in its original box, discovered at a 1997 *Antiques Roadshow*, and estimated at £15,000 to £20,000, sold at auction for £51,000.

The science fiction industry followed suit, with *Star Wars* figures, an instant cult with instant collectables. *Thunderbirds* (Dinky Toys' 1967 early Thunderbird 2 fetching over £120), *Doctor Who* (a 1968 battery-operated Dalek by Marx selling for around £80), *Wallace and Gromit*, with a whole range of merchandising from Shawn air fresheners to rucksacks, even the satirically aware creators of the Simpson family (look out for the Bart-Simpson-with-skateboard alarm clock) – all have signed up their images.

Being truly immortal, protected under extended copyrights, such characters have proved the movie industry's greatest investment. Word perfect, obedient, uncomplicated by agents, their potential, with 3-D computer graphics, seems infinite. Today, when Hollywood plans an animation film, executives think of the whole picture. No film illustrates this better than Pixar's classic, *Toy Story 2*. Voiced over by merely mortal Hollywood stars, the real celebrities (Woody and Buzz Lightyear) are shocked to find themselves on sale in the stores. The film ends and, in the cinema foyer on the way out, your children can buy the very celebrities they have just seen on screen. Smoke, mirrors and money: reality and fantasy fuse. What more could a collector want?

This porcelain sculpture of Michael Jackson and Bubbles by Jeff Koons fetched a world record price for a twentieth-century work of art: $5,615,750 in 2001. Will Jackson's fame endure – and will the work hold its value?

Nostalgia in a bubble: a Dinky Toy die-cast model of Thunderbird 2 (containing Thunderbird 4), in mint condition and in its original blister pack. A collector's dream and 'Ready to go . . . '

TIMELINE

The sports card market has its own fantasy rarity. The most desirable is the T206 Honus Wagner. In 1909, the cigarettes and card would have cost 50 cents. Astute early collectors in the 1950s would have been paying US$10, and by the 1960s, with collecting under way, the price would have been US$100. The field accelerated in the 1970s to US$1,000 plus, and, by the 1980s, to US$10,000, with the realisation of the card's rarity. In the 1990s, there was a cross-over of demand from both card and baseball collectors. One particular specimen, sold three times within nine years, made US$451,000 at Sotheby's in 1991, US$640,000 at Christie's in 1996 and around 2000, US$1,265,000 on eBay.

Sweet Caporal cigarette card of Honus Wagner from 1909. The first sports subject card to change hands for over US$1,000,000

CRYSTAL BALL

Ticking nearly all the right boxes comes the 'Top Gun' figure of President George W. Bush, available by mail order. It combines toy with icon, fact with fantasy, irony with adulation – a versatile must, whatever your politics. The blurb tells us that 'the figure captures the good ol' boy essence of the original George, from his rugged Texas back country good looks and characteristic placid political face. Its resemblance to the 43rd President is amazing, duplicating his crystal blue eyes, engaging smile and chiseled features.' Best of all, 'it's a fully poseable figure'.

Irony or adulation – you choose. The George W. Bush 'Top Gun' action figure

5

GRAHAM BUDD ON
SPORTING MEMORABILIA

TIM WONNACOTT

‘ Modest and self-effacing, keen and enthusiastic, Graham is a delightful man to work with. He is blessed with an encyclopaedic knowledge and tremendous experience. Since 1998, he has been head of the Sporting Memorabilia department at Sotheby's, having been with the company 25 years. I consider it a privilege to have been a colleague of Graham's over this period. „

In 2000 a golf club was purchased for 50p by a Lincolnshire golfer at a car boot sale. He could see that the look, proportions, weight and materials were highly unusual. It proved to be an eighteenth-century iron, made by an anonymous blacksmith who had wrought a heavy piece of iron into shape on his anvil to form the head and attached a thick, sturdy shaft of ash. The 50p investment yielded £5,200 when it was sold at Sotheby's in 2000, representing a staggering profit of 10,400 per cent.

Apart from relaying a wondrous moment of good fortune, the tale of the Lincolnshire golfer illustrates an important point in sporting memorabilia. Although he had little knowledge of golf collectables, or of antiques, his understanding of golf proved key to recognising an important historical item, and its resultant financial reward. At the core of appreciating items of sporting heritage lies a love of sport.

This is intended to encourage potential collectors. If you are foremost a sporting enthusiast, you already have the essential qualification. Sporting memorabilia is accessible, and not overburdened by the need for specialist academic or technical knowledge. And it does not require a deep pocket to build a collection of increasing authority and scope.

There is also the opportunity for reaping longer-term financial rewards in a popular collecting

A silver and enamel salver, Joseph Walton
& Co, London, 1928, commemorating the
1933 Ryder Cup at Southport & Ainsdale
GC; diameter 14 in/35.5 cm

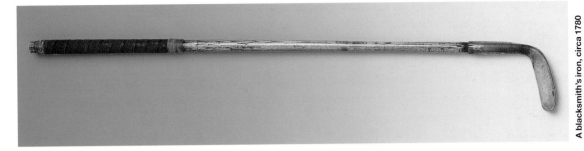

A blacksmith's iron, circa 1780

area. Recent slow economic growth, stock market depression, poor dividends and looming pension difficulties have turned many away from mainstream investments and encouraged them to seek alternative investment strategies, including collectables markets.

Worth stating here is some advice, appropriate to all sporting markets and universal to all areas of antiques and collectables. Firstly, rare or unusual items, from an early period, or in fine condition, will always be desirable. Quality is the easiest thing to market and sell. Whatever a collector's budget, it is best to invest in a few choice items rather than to spread the money thinly across lesser items.

A further point regards modern material offered as limited editions, prints or collectors' plates, for example. Often these commemorate memorable individuals or occasions and have a particular meaning for a prospective buyer. I would recommend their acquisition as a suitable memento. However, if investment is your motive, be far more cautious. The fact that they are produced as multiples lessens their chances of providing a lucrative return. Generally, the value of a limited edition on the secondary market is below the original retail price and likely to stay so for many years.

The prestigious end of the market often circles around items directly related to sportsmen's careers and their successes, marked by the presentation of medals, trophies and awards. In the case of football and cricket, interest extends to international caps, as well as kit and clothing such as shirts, boots and blazers and other keepsakes.

Paper collecting is a large sub-market and includes programmes, match tickets, autographs, photographs, postcards, books and many other general collectables.

FOOTBALL

Football collecting began to flourish in the 1990s, proving one of the fastest growing collectables areas over the past decade. In 2003 a gold 1888 FA Cup winner's medal, won by West Bromwich Albion's Charlie Perry, fetched £9,000. A medal won by another member of this West Brom side, Joe Wilson, was sold for £2,800 in 1989 (an increase of 321 per cent over 14 years). In 1991, a copy of the 1897 FA Cup final programme, between Aston Villa and Everton, made £1,600. Another copy of the programme was offered in 2003 and had climbed to £6,000 (an increase of 375 per cent over 12 years).

Underpinning the football market is its supreme popularity. It is difficult to envisage a time when football will not dominate the world of sport as it does today.

The prices in the football market are driven by the celebrity cult. Very high prices can be achieved for current stars, such as Beckham and Owen. These prices can rival those of historical figures in the game – in marked contrast to cricket, golf and tennis, where the emphasis is on golden age legends, such as Don Bradman, Old Tom Morris or Fred Perry.

Many theme their collection around the team they support, so Manchester United are top of the memorabilia league. It is a costly business to collect United items but you are sure to accumulate material that will always be in demand. In the post-war period, there are three sought after eras – the ill-fated Busby Babes team of the 1950s, the European Cup winning vintage of 1968 and Sir Alex Ferguson's 1999 Treble Winners.

The interest in World Cup memorabilia has accelerated quickly, with record auction prices for items such as Pelé's Brazilian jersey from the 1970 World Cup final, which fetched £140,000 in 2002. The fascination with the boys of 1966 remains undiminished. The price of a full set of World Cup squad signatures now bears comparison with those other 1960s icons, The Beatles. At a Sotheby's sale in 2003, a 1966 World Cup final programme fully signed by the England squad fetched £1,700.

A gold 1888 FA Cup winner's medal won by West Bromwich Albion's Charlie Perry

A 1966 World Cup programme fully signed by the England squad

GOLF

Golf is more established, with the first specialised golfing sale taking place in the early 1980s. There are many collectors in America where the sport is immensely popular. Japanese collectors became interested in the late 1980s/early 1990s and, for a short, glorious period preceding the Far East economic downturn, golf prices became highly inflated. In fact, memorabilia bought at the height of the market will often be worth less today. This is a cautionary tale, and a reminder that sporting memorabilia have the same characteristics as any other investment. The market can be cyclical and investments need to be viewed over extended periods. In this sense, golf represents a market that is currently favourable for buyers and has

room for prices to climb again.

The implements used dominate every golf auction. Golf clubs and balls have been manufactured with endless diversity over the years, offering collectors a wide range to assemble into an authoritative collection. The traditional skills of the club and ball maker are of Scottish origin.

Early golfers used the feather ball. These were balls stuffed with (goose) feathers, stitched inside a leather casing. Surviving examples are highly sought after and the world record price for such an object is £28,000.

Because of the feather ball's delicacy, the clubs employed were primarily made with wooden heads. Irons were only used sparingly. These wooden headed clubs are expertly crafted, beautiful objects,

From left to right, a Tom Morris, St. Andrews, long nosed long spoon, circa 1880, £2,400; a Tom Morris, St. Andrews, long nosed driver, circa 1870, £4,800; a Tom Morris, St. Andrews, long nosed long spoon, circa 1870, £4,000; a Robert Forgan, St. Andrews, long nosed brassie, circa 1885, £750; a Hugh Philp, St. Andrews, long nosed short spoon, circa 1840, £10,000

which make elegant display items. Referred to as long-nosed, they resemble a hockey stick rather than the modern day golf club. These quality clubs are sure to be desirable in the future, but can be expensive. So be selective and invest in examples in fine condition and stamped with makers' names.

During the second half of the nineteenth century, golf was revolutionised by the gutta percha ball, known as the gutty. Gutta percha was a rubber-like substance from the Far East that was moulded into a golf ball that could be made at a fraction of the cost of featheries and by less skilled workmen. Then, in 1898, the American inventor, Coburn Haskell, patented the rubber-core golf ball, which had a wound core of tensioned-rubber thread. The rubber ball travelled further through the air and, on landing, bounced and ran on – the gutty ball would virtually stop dead on the fairway. This led to the redesign of the golf club. A golfer needed a way of stopping the ball on the green when playing an iron approach shot. This was solved by the introduction of markings on the face of the iron from which the player could impart back spin. These markings varied from lines, dashes, dots and criss-crosses to many other types of scoring. Consequently, this is a way of identifying the age of an iron-headed club. The irons from the feather and gutty ball eras are smooth faced. If the implement has a marked face, then it is twentieth century and in all probability of no great significance, unless the club has an otherwise unusual feature or a patented innovation.

The long tradition of the wooden-shafted golf club ended in the 1930s when steel-shafted clubs were finally accepted. Invented in 1893 by Thomas Horsburgh of Edinburgh, they were not legalised by the Royal & Ancient Golf Club until 1929. Steel-shafted clubs are very largely ignored by collectors, who concentrate on the hickory shafted era. Attention may turn to these clubs in the future, but investment is only advised if you are prepared for a long-term speculation. The redeeming factor is that you can currently buy them for next to nothing.

CRICKET

Cricket auctions have been organised by the leading London auction houses since 1978. The market is far less international – the main collecting countries being the UK and Australia. Consequently, Ashes memorabilia can command a high price. Australian collectors first announced their arrival when the MCC held a sale of selected items from their spectacular collection during their bicentenary year, 1987. The state of any sporting market is influenced by events in the game. In recent years, the cricket market has become static in the UK, while it has enjoyed a boom in Australia, mirroring the relative disappointments and successes of the two nations. If the English game enjoys a revival, then cricketana at today's prices could look cheap.

1948 is often considered the landmark between the old and modern eras – being the year of Sir Donald Bradman's last tour of England with the Australian Invincibles team. The concentration of interest and prices is from the early era, and this still seems to be the vogue. Recently, the collections of players from the 1950s onwards have appeared at auction. The results in many cases were far from spectacular and cricket memorabilia from the second half of the twentieth century is woefully undervalued.

A cricket bat signed by the Australian Test tourists and a selection of County Sides, 1930, sold for £550

There must surely be room for growth in this area.

Cricket auctions can be dominated by books and *John Wisden's Cricketers' Almanack* is king. First published in 1864, these ever-popular annuals have always been desirable collector's items and still represent the backbone of many collections.

Autographs are highly sought after. For display, cricket bats signed by team groups are always popular. Go for those signed on full-size bats rather than the miniature bats, which yield less satisfactory results. Expect to pay more for Test teams than for county sides. Signed tour programmes, scorecards and itineraries also make fine collectables.

Whatever your sporting interest, there is a wealth of material. Collecting sporting memorabilia is a popular and fulfilling hobby which should repay your investment with attractive dividends over the longer term.

Resources

Further Reading
Football
Soccer Memorabilia, A Collectors' Guide, Graham Budd, Philip Wilson Publishers Ltd, 2000
Golf
Golf Implements and Memorabilia, David Neech, Philip Wilson Publishers Ltd, 1999

The Story of the Golf Ball, Kevin W. McGimpsey in association with Philip Wilson Publishers Ltd, 2003
The Encyclopaedia of Golf Collectables, John M Olman & Morton W Olman, Books Americana, 1985
Tennis
Racket Sports Collectables, Robert T Everitt, Schiffer Publishing Ltd, 2002
Tennis Antiques & Collectables, Jeanne Cherry, Amaryllis Press, 1995
Cricket
The Wisden Book of Cricket Memorabilia, Marcus Williams & Gordon Phillips, Lennard Publishing, 1990
Horse Racing
Horse Racing Art and Memorabilia, A Celebration of the Turf, Graham Budd, Philip Wilson Publishers Ltd, 1997

UK Sports Museums
The National Football Museum Preston
01772 908442 www.nationalfootballmuseum.com
The MCC Museum Lord's Cricket Ground, London NW8
020 7616 8656 www.mcc.org.uk
The British Golf Museum St Andrews, Fife
01334 460046 www.britishgolfmuseum.co.uk
Wimbledon Lawn Tennis Museum London SW19
020 8946 6131 www.wimbledon.org/museum
The Museum of Rugby Twickenham
020 8892 8877 www.rfu.com
The National Horseracing Museum Newmarket, Suffolk
01638 667333 www.nhrm.co.uk
The River and Rowing Museum Henley-on-Thames, Berks
01491 415600 www.rrm.co.uk

Collectors' Clubs
British Golf Collectors Society
www.britgolfcollectors.wyenet.co.uk
Cricket Memorabilia Society
www.cricket.org
Tennis Collectors Society
c/o Gerald Gurney, Guildhall, Great Bromley, Colchester, Essex CO7 7TU

TIMELINE

The desirability of *Wisden* as a collector's item offers a rare opportunity in sporting memorabilia of tracking the appreciation of Wisden prices for complete runs over an extended period. Some examples are:
1937, Sotheby's, £33 / 1954, Hodgson's, £145
1972, J.W. McKenzie, £750 / 1979, Philips, £4,200
1987, Philips, £14,940 / 2000, Sotheby's, £26,000

CRYSTAL BALL

A sport that has been something of a sleeping giant in memorabilia terms was rudely awoken by events in Sydney on 22 November 2003. The England team's triumph in the Rugby World Cup – the first English victory in a World Cup since the footballers of 1966 – sparked an immediate surge of interest in related memorabilia. Items such as signed shirts and rugby balls have become eagerly sought after. It would be no surprise to see this fascination with World Cup memorabilia spark interest in all items of rugby heritage. Rugby looks set fair to become the newest area of growth within sporting memorabilia, and steep rises in prices can be safely anticipated.

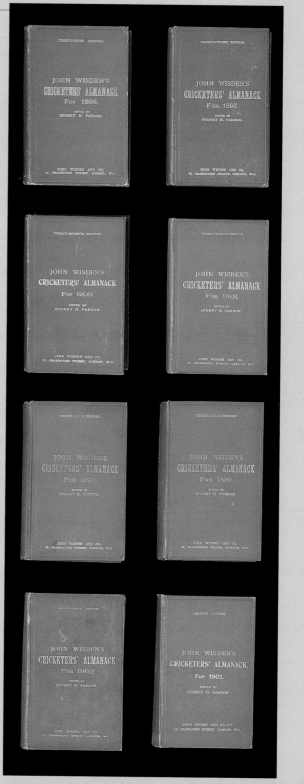

6

HILARY KAY ON ROCK AND ROLL MEMORABILIA

TIM WONNACOTT

" Hilary was one of the first people I met when I started at Sotheby's Belgravia saleroom in 1978. She was the (extremely) young head of the vibrant Collectors' Department which included dolls, costume and textiles, automata and mechanical music, kitchenalia and more. I was so glad to have had the chance to work with Hilary during those fun years. "

You can spend a few pounds or a few million to begin collecting rock memorabilia. The world record price for any rock and roll collectable is over US$2.25 million at a New York auction for John Lennon's psychedelic Rolls Royce. But don't be put off. Rock and roll collectables can include almost anything, from cars to T-shirts. Provided what you buy is directly connected to an individual rock musician or band, to a particular record, concert, film or event, your choice will be valid.

I came up with the idea of the first ever auction of rock and roll memorabilia in 1981. Held at Sotheby's in London, it launched a spectacularly successful new collecting area on to the auction market. Before 1981, there was no central point where rock memorabilia could be bought. I wanted to provide a venue for all those who were, like me, keen to see their passion for rock music and its stars recognised.

Luckily for my Sotheby's career, that first auction was a great success. Much to everyone's surprise, the sacred halls of Sotheby's, better known for Renoir and Fabergé, began to feature rock and roll memorabilia sales annually. I still noticed the occasional raised eyebrow from fellow

John Lennon's Phantom V Rolls Royce was painted in a riot of psychedelic rococo swags and cartouches by a fairground artist in 1967. Sold for US$2.25 million, Sotheby's New York, 1985

directors forced to rub shoulders with a new type of Sotheby client – rock fans dressed in jeans, sporting Mohican hairstyles.

The first sale's success became headline news and soon rock memorabilia auctions were held by other auctioneers internationally. To date, at Sotheby's alone, more than US$50 million worth of rock and roll memorabilia has been sold at auction. Rock memorabilia totalling tens of millions of dollars more has been sold through other auctioneers and dealers. More recently, the internet has proved a rich hunting ground, giving easy and cheap international access for a huge variety of material.

Rock memorabilia is now widely available. But the unscrupulous are tapping into the enthusiasm of collectors, and buyers must be extremely careful. Huge amounts of material in circulation include, at best, modern copies and, at worst, outright fakes. Do your homework before buying. Read up on the subject, go to conventions, buy auction catalogues, view the auction sales (perhaps the only opportunity for a novice to handle the best in the field), and speak to experts and established collectors.

Almost anything you could imagine is available. What you buy boils down to your wallet and your available space.

VEHICLES

Cars and other motor vehicles attract wide
interest from those with money and space.
Most desirable are those inextricably linked
to performers, such as Lennon's psychedelic
Phantom V Rolls Royce or ZZ Top's red hot-rod,
which appeared on album covers and videos.
The cross-pollination between car enthusiasts and
rock and roll devotees can lead to serious auction
room battles, when a buyer only interested in the
vehicle pits his bank balance against a dedicated
rock memorabilia collector.

MUSICAL INSTRUMENTS

Perhaps the most obvious collectable rock
icons are musical instruments associated with
particular performers, concerts, films, videos or
hit records – such as the white Fender Stratocaster
on which Jimi Hendrix performed his irreverent
version of 'The Star Spangled Banner' at the 1969
Woodstock festival. Such rare, iconic instruments
seldom appear in auction, and the results are
unpredictable when they do. The Hendrix
Woodstock Stratocaster was estimated at between
£60,000 and £70,000, but the hammer fell at the
extraordinary figure of £198,000 – the world
record for a rock guitar for over a decade. An
unsubstantiated rumour circulated that this
guitar was re-sold by that auction buyer for
around US$750,000 a couple of years later, and
the guitar now resides in a private collection
in Seattle.

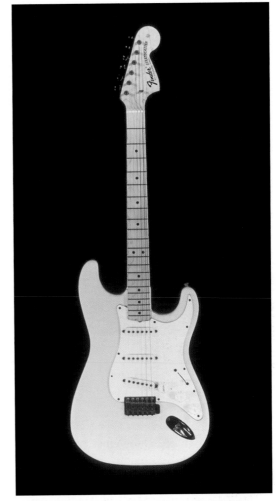

Jimi Hendrix's Fender Stratocaster guitar, used by Hendrix
at the Woodstock festival of 1969 and seen in the film of the
festival. The guitar was strung for left-hand play and saw
a lot of use – it displayed chips and dents on the body, and
burns on the headstock where Hendrix placed his cigarettes
and spliffs while he played

Madonna's underwear/outerwear costume from her 'Blond Ambition' tour of 1990, which made £9,000 at auction. Designed by Parisian couturier Jean Paul Gaultier, one of the gold corsets was offered as a first prize in a contest organised by MTV and Pioneer

Paul McCartney's handwritten lyrics for 'She's Leaving Home' from 1967, sold at auction for £41,000

COSTUME

Costumes made famous by concert or video performances, as well as trademark streetwear of rock personalities, occasionally appear on the market. These are generally bought by institutions or museums rather than individual collectors because of the difficulties in displaying costume. These did not deter enthusiasts who competed fiercely for Madonna's iconic gold lamé Jean Paul Gaultier outerwear/underwear corset worn for her 'Blond Ambition' tour. The price of around £9,000 looks, in retrospect, like a good buy, such is Madonna's continued standing. I would not bet that the £3,525 paid at auction in 2003 for Britney Spears' costume for her 'Oops, I Did It Again' tour of 2000 will stand a similar test of time.

MANUSCRIPTS

Dedicated collectors and, occasionally, museums are attracted by rare manuscript material, such as concert set lists, letters and original handwritten song lyrics. A set list (the order in which songs will be played in a concert), handwritten in black felt tip pen by Bob Dylan for an early 1990s concert, is one example. Including classic songs such as 'Lay Lady Lay', 'Rolling Stone' and 'Blowing in the Wind', it was valued at around £700 for auction in 2003. A fan paid £1,528 in 2003 for Phil Collins' complete lyrics for his 1985 number one 'Easy Lover'. However, the world record price for a piece of rock manuscript material is the staggering US$455,000 paid for the lyrics of The Beatles' song 'Nowhere Man'. Written in 1965 by John Lennon in black ballpoint ink, the lyrics were sold by Christie's in New York in 2003. Until then, the highest price for a manuscript lyric was the £161,000 paid in 1995 for 'Getting Better' from The Beatles' seminal album *Sgt. Pepper's Lonely Hearts Club Band*.

SIGNATURES

Owning a signature of a one's rock hero, whether on a blank piece of paper, on a publicity photograph, on a poster or a record is often a fan's ultimate goal. But this is an area most riddled with fakes and forgeries in rock memorabilia.

In the early 1960s, bands often asked members of their entourage to 'sign' items handed in at the stage door after a concert. Sometimes band members were skilled in signing for others in the band. I had a memorable conversation with Bill Wyman when he was viewing one of my rock memorabilia auctions at Sotheby's. Looking at a set of Rolling Stones' signatures in an autograph book and at my catalogue description which read 'signed by the Rolling Stones', Bill Wyman suggested that I change the entry to 'signed by the Rolling Stone'. He smilingly admitted that he had been responsible for signing not only his own name, but all the other members of the Stones as well!

POP ART

Original two-dimensional works of art are some of the easiest items to display successfully at home and are sought by individuals and by institutions interested in the design aspect of the piece, as well as by more specialised collectors of memorabilia. These two-dimensional images include paintings and self-portraits by performers, celluloids for

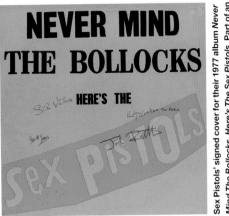

Sex Pistols' signed cover for their 1977 album *Never Mind The Bollocks, Here's The Sex Pistols*. Part of an orchestrated graphic campaign to shock and outrage

animated films, artwork for album covers, posters and photographs. It may be the fact that punk rock was short-lived that drives collectors to compete for the posters and printed material related to this music and style phenomenon. A concert poster for the Sex Pistols at the 100 Club, dating from 1976, realised over £3,000 at auction in 2001.

Many collectors regard photographs as works of art equivalent to original paintings. As a result, archive images or images completely new to the market can command extraordinary prices. One such was a group of 21 previously unpublished images of The Jimi Hendrix Experience performing in 1969 which were sold with copyright for over £14,000. Many collectors still seek the well-known, published images of their idols by the original photographers. Indeed, several professional photographers have become permanently associated with particular bands. Astrid Kirchherr, Jurgen Vollmer, Dezo Hoffman and Richard Avedon were each responsible for creating some of the best-known images of The Beatles from their Hamburg days in 1961 to their psychedelic 1967.

Gold disc presented to Keith Richards for *Exile on Main Street* by the Rolling Stones. These awards are scarce if presented to a member of the band who recorded the album – Keith Richards' name engraved on the brass plaque ensures this disc will hold its value

RECORD SALES

For sheer glamour, nothing beats the silver, gold and platinum records presented to the top selling performers for outstanding record sales. These awards look very impressive displayed in quantity on plain walls. When I visited Elton John in the late 1980s, several passageways in his home were hung floor to ceiling with just a small selection from his vast collection of personal record sales awards. Although discs presented to the performer responsible for the record are scarce and expensive, similar discs were given to other individuals involved with the recording project and these are more plentiful and correspondingly more affordable.

MERCHANDISE

Merchandise, generally meaning manufactured goods related to a popular performer or band, was produced in quantity from the 1960s onwards. It was then the easiest type of rock and roll memorabilia to collect because it could be bought over the counter in high street shops. Barbie-style dolls, wallpaper, curtains, blankets, rugs, plastic guitars, mugs, T-shirts, badges – all were available at the time the groups were popular. There was no need for fans to attend a concert or join a fan club to indulge their passion in a particular band. Vintage merchandise is relatively plentiful and, with a bit of careful hunting, can still be bought inexpensively.

A group of Beatles' merchandise dating from the mid-1960s which epitomises the rampant Beatlemania of the time. Including plates, wigs, stockings, material, tiles, badges and guitars, almost all of which could have been bought over the counter in high street shops – now highly sought after by collectors

BUILDING A COLLECTION

One of the easiest ways is to buy from a reputable dealer or auction house who guarantee the authenticity of the objects they sell. The internet now offers a number of auction sites for rock memorabilia, but seldom are these items offered with guarantees of authenticity. But there are many other ways to collect.

Actually attending a rock gig is the most obvious, with memorabilia often on sale which cannot be bought retail elsewhere. Occasionally, being in the right place at the right time plays a part. You can reap rewards by patiently standing at the stage door and obtaining signatures on your concert programme, poster or CD cover.

Conventions are excellent venues for buying or swapping to improve your collection or simply to meet fellow enthusiasts. These are held regularly and either focus on particular performers or take the form of second-hand and collectable record fairs which cover many types of music and different bands.

Charity auctions can also be a happy hunting ground when they include objects donated by performers personally. Kylie Minogue gave a pair of trousers she wore for the promo video for her single 'Never Too Late' to a Comic Relief charity auction in 1991. Britney Spears donated a large number of items for an on-line auction in May 2003 to raise money for her charity, The Britney Spears Foundation. The buyers knew that Kylie's trousers and everything from Britney's sale came with an impeccable provenance.

Private individuals have always played a significant role in the market. They include those influenced directly by the performers the first time around, as well as a new generation of younger collectors who have just discovered a particular band or style of music. At memorabilia conventions and auction previews, some will be dedicated fans who view every lot carefully and buy selectively, while others may simply buy on impulse for themselves or to give as presents.

When rock memorabilia was first offered for sale at auction there were few dealers. Now, it is a different story, with many more dealers active today, and their impact on the market has become more significant.

Commercial enterprises are unpredictable buyers and their importance in the market can fluctuate widely from one year to the next; sometimes a radio or television station, a restaurant or a newspaper will buy in order to use the memorabilia as a publicity vehicle to attract customers. Often, once they have what they want, these commercial buyers disappear completely, leaving scarcely a ripple, and allowing fans and enthusiasts their rightful place at the heart of rock memorabilia collecting.

Resources

Further reading

Rock 'n' Roll Collectables – An Illustrated History of Rock Memorabilia, Hilary Kay, Simon & Schuster, 1992

The Beatles – A Guide to Memorabilia, Stephen Maycock, Apple Press, 1997

All the King's Things, Bill Yenne, Bluewood Books, 1994

Rolling Stones Album, Geoffrey Giuliano, Penguin USA, 1993

Christie's Rock and Pop Memorabilia, Hodgson & Doggett, Pavilion Books Ltd, 2003

TIMELINE

Signed photographs of the Rolling Stones have risen in price gradually over the years (£71 in 1983, £200 in 1990 and £764 in 2003). But The Beatles have proved to be an amazing investment. In 1982 a signed Beatles photograph could have been bought for £280, which rose to £880 in 1990 but in 2003 a signed Beatles photograph was sold at auction for a staggering £4,465.

A black and white photograph signed by all four members of The Beatles. The original was almost certainly taken during a photo session shot by Dezo Hoffman, responsible for some of the best-known images of The Beatles in the early 1960s

CRYSTAL BALL

Tips for future collecting of rock memorabilia are not easy. Record companies themselves hardly know whether their acts are likely to stand the test of time. I would urge caution. Only spend money on individuals or bands which have been internationally successful for at least five years, have the backing from a well-established record company, have won international music awards and enjoy the support of an active and flourishing international fan base.

A collection of signed memorabilia relating to a new-ish British band that has a wide international following and which has stood the ten-year time test. Dating from 1994, this kind of memorabilia was relatively easy to obtain during the early days of the band

7

MADELEINE MARSH ON
FASHION: CLOTHING AND ACCESSORIES

TIM WONNACOTT

I met Madeleine when we were presenting *The BBC Antiques Show* and we now work together regularly on the *Antiques Roadshow*. Madeleine is an 'original', colourful both in dress and character. Some might call her zany, but she's a lady with opinion and an expert who is constantly breaking new ground in the exciting world of fashion.

When asked what I collect for myself, I rustle my multi-coloured net petticoats, click my stilettos and stretch out my flowery 1950s circle skirt. 'I collect vintage fashion,' I reply proudly. 'Isn't this a great frock?'

I am not alone in my passion. At the Oscars, leading actresses now regularly step out in vintage Valentino and Dior. In fashion magazines, the latest designer look is often set off with antique accessories. Vintage fashion stores and markets are places where you can find yourself rubbing shoulders with 'it' girls from *Hello!* and with fashion designers in search of inspiration. Vintage fashion has even hit the high street. In London's Oxford Street, Selfridge's has a vintage clothes department, Top Shop sells 1960s and 1970s originals and John Lewis stocks vintage costume jewellery.

The great joy of collecting fashion and accessories is that you can take them out and show them off. Clothes also provide a direct link with the past. Try on an Edwardian coat, a 1920s flapper dress, a 1950s New Look ball gown or a 1960s mini skirt, and you look, feel and even walk differently. Most costume collectors focus on a specific period that suits their personality and their figure. 1920s enthusiasts are often small and slight, 1950s fans are frequently curvaceous, whilst 1960s dressers tend to be enviably long, lean and leggy.

Some people dress completely in period style, whilst others, myself included, mix and match old and new. You can team a 1950s shirt with a pair of jeans, a 1920s coat with a modern dress.

Vintage fashion is fun to collect and wear and, if well chosen and well looked after, can be a good investment. A 1920s black jet beaded evening dress that I bought for £25 in the 1980s is now worth twenty times that. A more recent favourite purchase is a 1950s dress, picked up a from a charity shop for a fiver. A lovely print, handmade, beautifully boned, with stiffened underskirt, the same frock might cost me £80 to £100 from a vintage fashion dealer. My sense of having found a collectable bargain enhances my pleasure in wearing the frock.

GETTING STARTED

If you are buying vintage to wear, as with modern fashion, buy what suits you and what you feel good in. And, as with all other collectables, buy what you like.

Always try clothes on. Some period clothes are too small for modern-day wearers, while others were designed for a level of corsetry that we do not encounter today. Too big is not necessarily a problem, since garments can be adapted or taken in, but too small is always a bad idea, as ancient textiles do not take kindly to straining.

Condition is crucial. Check hems, seams, fastenings, underneath the arms, anywhere a garment may have become torn or worn. Some

damage is easy to mend, but more serious faults can be irreparable; sometimes material just disintegrates with age. If you're good at sewing, you can carry out your own minor repairs. If not, you will need help. Ask your nearest vintage clothes dealer to recommend a dry cleaner – preferably the one they use – both for mending and cleaning. A cleaner with experience with vintage or theatrical costumes, who won't iron out your Fortuny-style pleats or nuke your sequins, is a real advantage.

Condition is also important for its future collectability. Care for your outfits, and they will last to be worn and enjoyed by future generations.

WHERE TO SHOP

Charity shops are good places to look: one of my recent purchases was a 1970s Ossie Clark shirt, which cost me £5 from Oxfam. There are specialist vintage fashion dealers and many antique centres have a small clothing section. You will find classic designer outfits at vintage fashion fairs and specialist auctions. A period Pucci or Schiaparelli, or some other big name couturier creation, however, will cost you hundreds, even thousands of pounds, rather than a fiver.

Big antiques markets are also good, perhaps most famously Portobello Market in London. Since the fashion section is mostly outdoors, this does involve some ingenuity when trying things on. I have changed in the back of a car, in a local café's loo, and underneath a dealer's table.

WHAT TO WEAR?

The twentieth century offers a wealth of styles. Every decade has its treasures and its ideals of female beauty, some more accessible and wearable than others.

1900s

Edwardian ladies aspired to an S-shaped silhouette: bosom thrust forward, tiny waist, hips and bottom pushed back, an exaggerated feminine line maintained by viciously controlling corsets. Hair piled high was supplemented with false hairpieces to support large picture hats, decorated with ribbons, flowers, feathers and even stuffed birds.

Although this is not a look for many modern women, the Edwardian period does offer some wearable fashion. White lawn muslin and lace day dresses were in every girl's wardrobe. Comparatively loose fitting, these make lovely summer dresses and can be found from around £200. Elaborate brocade housecoats, and outdoor coats produced for new crazes, such as motoring, are another option.

Accessories, however, provide perhaps the easiest way of adopting a bit of *fin de siècle* style. Hat-pins, necessary to secure those towering hats, and made out of every conceivable material, are interesting collectables. Values depend on medium, maker and style. A simple example in non-precious metals might cost you under £10. A silver hat-pin by British Art Nouveau jeweller Charles Horner could be worth £50 to £80. Rare novelty designs command high prices – I recently saw an Edwardian hat-pin with the top in the form of a tiny silver bicycle selling at a dealer's for £195. If you want to go for big names (and spend

A drawstring bag with finely woven beads and floral decoration, c. 1900

thousands), Fabergé and Lalique also produced hat-pins.

Popular with collectors today, Victorian and Edwardian handbags can be found made from beads, tapestry and silver mesh. Fine examples sell for £200 to £300. Though they can be too fragile for anything but the most delicate occasional use, they look beautiful hung from the wall as display items.

Austrian Petit Point bag, floral decoration with gilt metal and cornelian clasp, 1930s

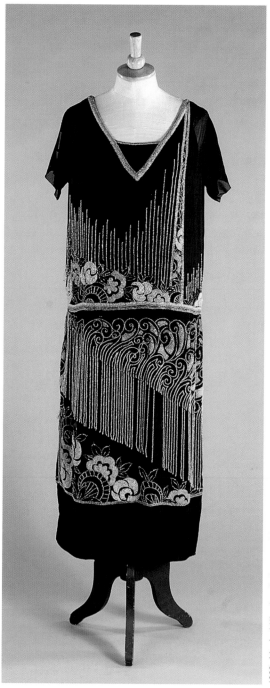

1920s black chiffon beaded gown with pink and clear crystal beadwork fringes and motifs

1920s and 1930s

The 1920s flapper shingled her hair, shortened her skirts, and cast off her corset in favour of a straight, boyish silhouette that mirrored the streamlined modernism of Art Deco. Arguably the best and most collectable example of 1920s style is the beaded shift dress, which epitomised the Charlestoning spirit of the jazz age. Thanks to their loose drop-waisted line, these dresses fit the modern figure and still look magnificently glamorous. Good examples sell for £1,000 and more, and, as a design classic, will never go out of fashion. Condition is crucial to value, however. These dresses are hand-sewn with hundreds of beads and sequins. If you rip an encrusted panel, you leave a trail of beads like a decorative snail. The beads' weight can also cause fine chiffon to rip, so dresses are best stored flat, rather than on hangers.

Interwar lamé evening coats and jackets are

also timeless classics (I wear my 1920s metallic thread coat with jeans). In the 1920s and 1930s, soft and beautiful silk pile velvet was used. It has a lovely sheen, and develops a lustrous patina with age. More summery purchases include the silk and lace slips, and the bias-cut, printed chiffon gowns, which were worn over this luxurious lingerie. Buyer beware, however. The bias cut is elegant and feminine, but only if you have the right figure. As with all vintage fashion, prices depend on where you buy. A fine 1930s dress could cost you £200 to £300 or more from a fashionable, metropolitan vintage clothes store, but you can make cheaper finds in street markets.

1940s and 1950s

During the Second World War, women's clothes echoed men's uniforms – tight suits with crisp lines and short skirts using as little material as possible. Underwear was made from parachute silk, and, unable to get stockings, women painted their legs brown and drew seams with eyebrow pencils. Wartime shortages led to the creation of the Utility Scheme to provide essential clothing. Wares were marked with the CC41 trademark – standing for civilian clothing 1941, the year the scheme was launched. There is considerable interest today in these emergency fashions. Forties clothes are collected by Second World War

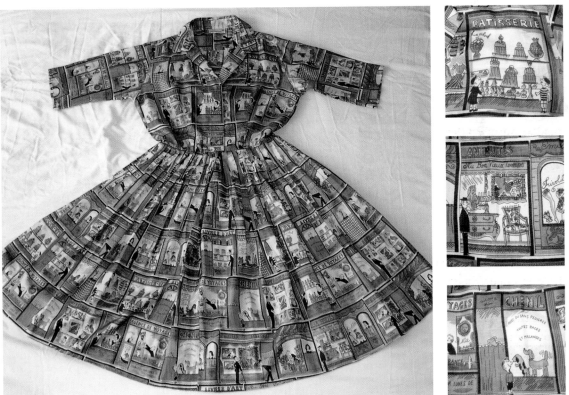

1950s American silk dress printed with Parisian shops

An Ossie Clark/Celia Birtwell printed chiffon ensemble c. 1969

enthusiasts, and by swing and jive fans, who like to dress up in period style for dances. A friend of mine who collects 40s clothes spent about £100 on her wartime WVS (Women's Voluntary Service) winter coat in regulation green. She also paid about £70 for a pair of imitation snakeskin shoes (complete with utility mark on the sole) in such perfect condition that she will only ever wear them on carpeted floors.

Shortages continued after the war. In Britain, things were at their very worst when, in 1947, Christian Dior launched his new look in Paris: padded jackets emphasising bust and hips, waist-whittling corsetry, and, most shocking of all, long swirling skirts using yards of material. 'I brought back the neglected art of pleasing,' claimed Dior. What he also brought back was the hourglass shape (reinforced by controlling underwear) and the desire to look like a woman. Couture clothes by designers such as Dior and Balenciaga sell for high prices. More affordable and easy to wear are mass-produced, cotton New Look style frocks. These cheerful and often very well-made dresses range in price from around £10 to over £100, depending on style and where you buy them. Much is readily available for under £50.

1960s and 1970s

In the 1960s and 1970s London was swinging. Twiggy, sixteen years old, weighing 91 lbs and with a cockney accent, established the look – skinny, leggy and breathtakingly young. Mary Quant pioneered a host of new female styles from mini skirts to boots, to trouser suits. British pop stars, such as The Beatles, The Rolling Stones and The Kinks, provided new male fashion icons, and Carnaby Street, centre of the peacock revolution

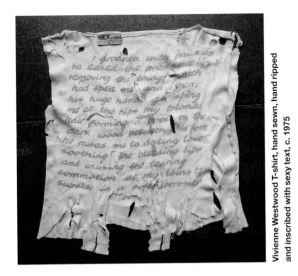

Vivienne Westwood T-shirt, hand sewn, hand ripped and inscribed with sexy text, c. 1975

in men's dress, became world famous.

Look out for labels of big name London designers and trendy boutiques. Paris, too, was shaken by the youthquake. Designers such as Cardin and Courreges launched the white and silver space age look. Paco Rabanne experimented with new materials, creating chain-mail dresses from plastic and metal. These 'sculptures' marked the advent of provocative, *avant garde*, and fundamentally unwearable clothes, designed to publicise the designer's name and attract attention to more profitable mass-market creations, such as perfume and ready to wear fashions. 'Haute Couture is dead,' sniffed Balenciaga as he closed his fashion house in 1968.

In the late 1960s and early 1970s the maxi took over from the mini and the Afghan coat from the plastic mac, giving a more romantic, dreamy look. London designers, such as Barbara Hulanicki at Biba and Ossie Clark, looked back to Art Nouveau and Art Deco, reinterpreting vintage styles with psychedelic colour and glamour. Glam was a 1970s

feature, with shiny disco clothes, towering platform boots and billowing flares adopted by men and women. The decade ended with punk. The bondage trousers and ripped-up T-shirts created by Vivienne Westwood are now hotly contested for in the saleroom by rock and pop enthusiasts, and can fetch as much as £1,000 apiece.

Every decade produces collectable fashion. Fine works by big designer names will always carry a premium. Clothes can be collectable because they epitomise their period, or because – like a 1920s flapper dress – they are simply lovely to wear.

Go to a party in a period outfit and no one will be wearing the same dress. People will almost certainly ask you about it. An antique dress, or even just a vintage handbag, can be a great icebreaker. The best thing about collecting vintage fashion is the pleasure of wearing it, and pleasure is what collecting – and dressing up – should be all about.

Resources

Further reading

Miller's Collecting the 1950s, Madeleine Marsh, Miller's Publications, 1997
Miller's Collecting the 1960s, Madeleine Marsh, Miller's Publications, 1999
Miller's Collecting Fashion and Accessories, Carol Harris, Miller's Publications, 2000
Shoes: A Celebration of Pumps, Sandals, Slippers and More, Linda O'Keeffe, Workman, 1996
Handbags: The Power of the Purse, Anna Johnson, Workman, 2002

Where to buy vintage fashion:

Major auction houses all hold occasional sales dedicated to fashion and there are also vintage fashion fairs.

Street markets

Portobello Market, Portobello Road London W11 (underneath the Westway) (Friday and Saturday)
Camden Market, Chalk Farm Road NW1 (Saturday and Sunday)
Greenwich Market, Greenwich Church Street, London SE1 (Saturday and Sunday)

Antique markets

Alfie's Antiques Market, London NW8 T: 020 7723 6066

Grays Antiques Market, London W1 T: 020 7269 7212

Dealers

Bohemia, Accrington Lancs T: 01254 231119

Circa, London SW6 T: 020 7736 5038
www.circavintage.com

Echoes, Todmorden, West Yorks T: 01706 817505

Orsini, London W8 T: 020 7937 2903

Rellik, London W10 T: 020 8962 0089

Twentieth Century Fashion T: 01342 840 765
www.c20vintagefashion.co.uk

What the Butler Wore, London SE1 T: 020 7261 1353

TIMELINE

As a student in the 1980s, I bought a fabulous 1920s black jet beaded evening dress for £25, which over the years has taken me through innumerable May balls and parties, together with an Art Deco evening coat for £20. Today, the same items might sell for over £500 apiece.

1920s evening coat, black silk embroidered with gilt metal thread, fur trim and finely embroidered lining in contrasting coffee colour

CRYSTAL BALL

Lulu Guinness is one of Britain's most famous handbag designers. Inspired by vintage examples and outrageously pretty, her creations appeal to enthusiasts of both retro and modern chic. Her handbags have been acquired by a number of museums and by celebrity fashionistas including Jerry Hall, Kylie Minogue, Kate Moss and Demi Moore. As well as producing more general lines, Lulu Guinness also makes a range of limited edition, collectable bags, each one numbered and hand detailed. My modern choice for a collectable of the future is a Lulu Guinness handbag, because it will always be usable and I can't imagine a time when women won't be seduced by its whimsical and charming design.

A Lulu Guinness diamante fan clutch bag, covered with Swarovski crystals

8

DAVID BATTIE ON
ORIENTAL CERAMICS

TIM WONNACOTT

'Mention the *Antiques Roadshow* and the face most people will conjure up is David's. For example, when we were truffling for bargains together recently in antique shops in Tallin in Estonia, David was recognised three times in the street by excited Estonians! Twenty-five years ago, he gave me my first job at Sotheby's Belgravia. He, therefore, has great taste and discernment (!), for where would I be today had he not given me my chance?'

CHINESE PORCELAIN

The long ruling Qing monarchy was abolished in 1912 and China became a republic under a president, Yuan Shikai. Porcelain, often of superb quality, was made in Jingdezhen at this time. Some of it bears Yuan Shikai's name or that of his short-lived reign as the Emperor Hongxian. There is no doubt that pieces from the first half of the century will rocket up in price, particularly those by major painters, who are beginning to be identified. The Chinese are already taking them very seriously.

With the exception of the early pieces, much twentieth-century Chinese porcelain is repetitive and uninspiring. However, there was a high spot under Mao when fascinating vases, dishes and figures were painted and sculpted depicting contemporary Chinese life, idealised workers and Mao himself. These rare pieces are of historical significance, given the importance of the period.

China is likely to be the major 21st-century economy. Already mainland buyers rival those from Taiwan and expats for early porcelain – they will surely move to later pieces as the earlier ones become almost unobtainable. The brave punter could go for vases and dishes made loosely in the style of eighteenth-century famille-rose (porcelain with a pinky hue) in the last twenty years for export. Examples, often found in their original

A Chinese famille-verte garden seat, circa 1975, 18in, £150–£180

A Chinese mallet-form porcelain vase, circa 1930, enamelled and gilt with precious objects and flowers on cell diaper, 8 1/4in, spurious seal mark of Qianlong (1736–1795), £80–£120

boxes and usually of almost eggshell quality, can be well painted and cheap for what they are.

More controversially, I would tip the recent mass-produced Canton porcelain simulating, but not copying exactly, eighteenth-century famille-rose, famille-verte, Canton and Japanese Imari. The decoration of garden seats, massive jardinières or fish bowls or vases is transfer printed in a smoky black and then infilled in colour. They are everywhere and inexpensive; a small bowl is under £20.

A Chinese cloisonné box and cover, early twentieth century, 3 1/8in, £15 with slight chips, £25–£30 perfect

CHINESE CLOISONNÉ

Nineteenth-century Chinese cloisonné is bought mostly for its decorative value. In the twentieth century, similar objects were made, particularly shallow bowls with incurved rims, a dragon curling round the well. They invariably have the mark *ta Ming nian zhi* (made in the Ming dynasty) on the underside and black and yellow were popular colours. These can be bought for £20 to £30. They are not bad quality and are probably a good buy. Better may be the large animals and birds, particularly cockerels, which were often gifts to diplomats or businessmen who had worked in China. Dismissed by the market as modern without considering their quality or decorative merit, they will still cost several hundreds of pounds but would definitely prove a good long-term investment.

CHINESE IVORIES

Ivory carvings have been found in Chinese tombs three thousand years old. The Chinese traditionally produced religious figures of Daoist, Confucian or Buddhist significance. In the late nineteenth century, these were repetitious and of little merit. There was a renaissance of inventive carving after the First World War, and during the Mao years when evocative and skilful carvings were made of workers, soldiers and peasants. Despite being created for the despised west, they generated much-needed cash for the régime. They were expensive at the time and are not common, but if they turn up in a local auction, they may be dismissed as modern and fetch only a decorative price. They are well worth looking out for and a strong tip for the future.

I would not tip chess sets. In elaborate wooden cases lined in velvet, many are, in fact bone, not ivory (or even plastic). Nor would I buy the intricately pierced temples, bridges and idealised 'heavens' which, although at first sight displaying extraordinary carving skills, are actually mechanically drilled and boring. These usually come in glass cases. However, the glass case *can* house skilful carving. Best are studies of flowers or, for example, a Chinese cabbage with a cricket on top. The feelers and legs of the insect are as thin as thread and the whole will be brightly coloured. These cost from around £200.

For the last 30 years, the Chinese in Hong Kong and elsewhere have been carving ivory *netsuke*, the toggles worn at the belt by the Japanese and never used by the Chinese. These bear signatures, often filled in black or red. One can find a hundred or so at a fair at prices of £20 upwards. They can be recognised by a slight pink cast to the colour of the ivory, a far-too-shiny surface and subject matter not tackled by the Japanese. An erotic one can be safely discounted – the originals are very rare.

There are several points about these carvings. The first is that the international CITES Convention protects endangered species, including the elephant. Any purchase of modern ivory may encourage illegal culling. Secondly, there are copies cast from the originals in plastic which are extremely difficult to detect – including similar carvings in wood which fooled me for a long time. Thirdly, I have dismissed them as worthless imitations, but am revising my opinion. Some of them are very skilfully done and show considerable humour and invention. Anyone could put together a collection which would probably pay dividends eventually but, frankly, you would have to steel yourself against your conscience.

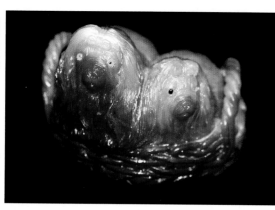

A Chinese agate group of two Pekinese in a basket, 4 in, late twentieth century, £100–£150

CHINESE SILVER

Prices for neglected nineteenth-century Chinese silver have recently begun to rise and there is still scope for twentieth-century pieces. The best examples date from the years up to the 1930s. Most common are tea sets with dragon handles and spouts, or in the form of lotus leaves. If you fancy collecting them, they are terrific value: £150 will buy a reasonable three-piece set. More popular are sets of spoons, often of flower form, which spoon collectors love, costing from £30 a set upwards. Other pieces, particularly two-handled cups, were made for presentation to the British in the Far East. These bear inscriptions and dates commemorating events such as boat races and cricket matches.

CHINESE HARDSTONES

Personally, I can't get terribly excited about jade. Carving may be very clever, as jade is at the upper end of the Moh scale (a test for hardness of natural materials), but the end result is always cold and unresponsive. However, good pieces have been made in the twentieth century. The introduction of electric-driven, diamond-encrusted drill bits has meant that 'carving' times have been greatly reduced. Costs have come down and less skilled workers can produce passable results. I have seen some very recent carvings of animals that are as charming as anything Fabergé did. Carnelian and agate seem to be popular stones and the natural coloration can be cleverly used. As always, the acutely tuned buyer can cherry-pick the goodies. The major danger here is not knowing whether one is handling jade itself or something else. Most common substitute is soapstone or stained talc. The latter is so soft it can be scratched with the fingernail and one should always upend a 'jade' and examine the base. Any sign of white lines or scuffing means a lesser stone. For a talc carving one should not pay much more than £30.

JAPANESE CERAMICS

On the *Antiques Roadshow*, one class of porcelain exceeds all others by a factor of ten: Japanese eggshell. It was made at Kutani and Nagoya in indescribable quantities and came to Europe and America by the shipload. I'm afraid we have to tell owners that a service is worth under £1 a piece – including those with a geisha head in the well. But, there is the occasional, uncommon, eggshell service that is well, if not brilliantly, decorated. The market dismisses all eggshell; seek out the good examples and one can buy something of merit for very little. Their time will come.

Some good Satsuma was made into the twentieth century, but standards were beginning to slip. These pieces are expensive for what they are and are best avoided.

A Seida eggshell porcelain saucer, circa 1930, transfer-printed and painted with cranes, printed mark. The coral-coloured dots are characteristic of the period, £2 (not recommended); a fine Takasaka plate painted with pheasant, circa 1920, 8 ⅜ in, red painted mark, £100–£150; a very rare eggshell coffee can and saucer by Shoko Takebe for Thomas B. Blow (a dealer/collector) and dated Meiji 40 (1907), £200–£300

The Fukagawa factory continued over the 1900 barrier making well-designed, well-decorated porcelain. Datelines may be difficult to determine; their early work can look almost Art Deco at times. Fukagawa rocketed up in price in the 1980s, but is now a bit quiescent. If you can find it reasonably priced, buy it.

Kutani porcelain, made in Kaga province, is underpriced, whether from the nineteenth or twentieth century. The palette of iron red, black and gold is unfashionable. As with everything else, there are appallingly bad pieces and there are great pieces, so be selective.

JAPANESE PRINTS

Japanese colour wood block prints from the eighteenth and nineteenth centuries, particularly those by the great masters, can make thousands. The Japanese continued woodblock printing as an artistic medium and these prints are fascinating snapshots of their time – the 1920s and 1930s being the best. Make sure the print has full margins and has not been trimmed, that it has not been folded or scuffed, and that the colours are bright. Twentieth-century prints will be signed in the margin by the artist who may well have cut the block and even done the printing himself. Expect to pay from £100 upwards.

A Japanese silver ring box, circa 1920, chased with chrysanthemums, 3 1/8 in., stamped jun gin and maker's mark in a triangle, £100–£200

JAPANESE CLOISONNÉ

The cloisonné made in Japan during the last two decades of the nineteenth century is unequalled by anyone, including the famous Fabergé. The best pieces can make tens of thousands of pounds and are beyond the pocket of all but the richest collectors. But there is a wide gap between these, usually signed, pieces and the rest. If bought for their decorative appeal, a pair of twelve-inch vases cost a couple of hundred pounds, and much, much less if one is prepared to tolerate some damage, as cloisonné is all but unrestorable.

JAPANESE SILVER

In the twentieth century, the Japanese used silver to make cigarette cases, and also cigarette and cigar boxes. These were either stamped or hand beaten, often with an abundance of flowers, and are decorative and good quality. The large boxes can be used for jewellery, or even tea bags; expect to pay £120 upwards. Cigarette cases, however, can be bought for £15 or so. More palatable are vases and bowls – again the chrysanthemum is common here – which were given frequently as gifts to foreigners working in Japan. Some even bear the Meiji Emperor's *kiku mon*, the stylised chrysanthemum badge, for diplomatic or high ranking recipients. Japanese silver will bear the characters *jun gin* (pure silver) and a maker/sponsor's name.

JAPANESE IVORIES

While true *netsuke* had been dispensed with when the Japanese adopted Western suits in the 1870s, they were still carved for sale in Europe and America in stores such as Liberty's. Larger groups (*okimono*), appealing to Western taste, largely supplanted the stock-in-trade of the *netsuke* carver. *Okimono* can range from a couple of inches to several feet, the larger examples obviously being sectional. The quality of the carving can be breathtaking and they will undoubtedly stand the test of time, sensitivity towards their origin notwithstanding. Prices start at £60 and can finish in the thousands for major examples. Some appealing studies of fruit were made – bananas the most common (£100), highly naturalistic and appropriately coloured. With the exception of a few netsuke artists working to traditional formulae, ivory carving was virtually over in Japan by the 1930s.

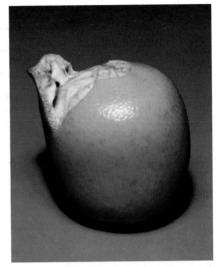

A Japanese ivory satsuma, early twentieth century, naturalistically carved and coloured, 2 ¹/₂ in, signed Seizan, £200–£300

A Japanese cloisonné vase, early twentieth century, with raised enamel in moriage technique by Ando Jubei, 14 ³/₈ in, stamped jun gin and inlaid seal, £8,000–£10,000

Resources

There are no internet sites, price guides, dealers, galleries or salerooms dedicated to twentieth-century Oriental ceramics. Some museums, such as the Victoria & Albert Museum, London SW7 (020 7942 2000) may have some twentieth-century pieces on display. Exhibitions by their nature are transitory, but some have produced worthwhile catalogues (see Further reading).

Further reading

Japan

Imperial Japan: The Art of the Meiji Era (1868–1912), Herbert F Johnson Museum of Art, Cornell University, NY, 1980*

Meiji: Japanese Art in Transition, Haags Gemeentenmuseum, 1987*

Japanese Imperial Craftsmen: Meiji Art from the Khalili Collection, Victor Harris, British Museum, 1994*

Satsuma, Masterpieces from the World's Important Collections, Louis Lawrence, 1991 (out of print, but available on Amazon)

Japanese Cloisonné, L A Coben and D C Ferster, Weatherhill, NY and Tokyo, 1982

China

From the Dragon's Treasure, Chinese Porcelain of the 19th & 20th Century, Gunhild Avitabile, Bamboo Publishing, 1987*

Heavenly Pieces, Peter Wain, 1993*

*Exhibition Catalogue

TIMELINE

A Kinkozan beaker vase painted by Shisui, 9 in, early twentieth century. When new, this vase would not have been cheap. The few original bills I have seen suggest that in real terms it might have cost about £500. By the mid-twentieth century, it had collapsed in value and was then, in real terms, worth only a few pounds. It sold in 1995 for £3,000 and would be unchanged today.

CRYSTAL BALL

The twentieth century is a plum ripe for picking. Concentrate on quality and condition and pieces that speak of the period in which they were made and one cannot go wrong. The Noritake coffee set is 1960s – the bright orange is a give-away – and it comes from a rapidly rising factory. Around £5 a piece now, but a sure-fire winner. Noritake from earlier in the century (the Edwardian pieces with landscapes and gilding in European taste) are already doing well but the minimalist taste on the rise will ensure that post-mid-century Noritake will leap up.

9

JAMES STRANG ON TWENTIETH-CENTURY DESIGN

TIM WONNACOTT

‟I came across James at an Edinburgh antiques fair. His stand was filled with some of the things I love – Christopher Dresser metal work and ceramics and glass designed by Keith Murray. As a designer, James explains, time spent understanding design sources is never wasted.„

Twentieth-century design is unlike any other collecting field. The most common misconception regarding the value of modern design is to confuse intrinsic value with design value. The latter is based on the designer, rarity and condition, and the ideological context of an item. What you are collecting is representative of a set of ideas: for example, a Keith Murray vase embodies the modernist ethos which informed his design. A vase designed by Clarice Cliff, although extremely popular and very much of its time, does not.

For his Royal College of Art degree show in 1981, Argentinian-born Daniel Weil designed the 'Radio in a Bag', which made us question the function of objects by breaking them down to their key components to create, in Weil's own words, 'a new imagery for electronics to escape from the mechanical imagery of the box'. This 'Radio in a Bag' can now be worth more than a Cartier watch. Now surprisingly difficult to find, a good example might fetch between £500 and £700 at auction.

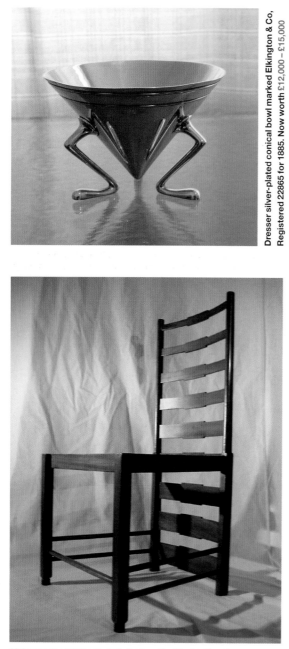

Dresser silver-plated conical bowl marked Elkington & Co, Registered 22865 for 1885. Now worth £12,000 – £15,000

Mahogany Ladderback chair designed by Charles Rennie Mackintosh circa 1917 for Derngate, Northampton. This chair was exhibited in '50 Years of Modern Design' at Bethnal Green Museum, London 1966. Value approximately £20,000 – £25,000

THE PURSUIT OF BEAUTY

There is a thread linking the designs from 130 years ago of Dr Christopher Dresser, who has been described as the father of modern design, with those of today.

Born in 1834, Dresser trained at the Government School of Design, before setting up a design studio. His students included Archibald Knox, who went on to design the Tudric and Cymric range of pewter and silverware for Liberty's. (Today, you may be able to buy a piece of Knox's pewter for less than £500, although his silverware can be more expensive. A rare decanter recently made £40,000 at auction.)

Dresser's interest in the aesthetics of Japanese and Peruvian decorative art is reflected in his designs, as is his background in botany. He was a man of his time, and fully understood all aspects of the manufacturing process. He championed the 'form follows function' doctrine decades before the modernists of the 1920s.

Dresser was associated with many firms, among others, Hukin & Heath for plate and silver; Linthorpe for ceramics; and Jas Coupar & Sons' Clutha range of glass. A silver-plated conical bowl, made for Elkington & Co in 1885, and marked 'Designed by Dr C Dresser', is now worth £12,000 to £15,000.

WHAT MODERN WAS

The 1900s heralded the age of the architect-designer, most of whom worked in Classical, Arts and Crafts, and Art Nouveau styles. They had complete autonomy over their projects, designing everything from a teaspoon in the dining room to a ridge tile on the roof.

One of the originals was Glaswegian architect and designer Charles Rennie Mackintosh, who, like Dresser, was influenced by Japanese art and design. His work inspired architects and designers in Germany and Austria. Vienna in the 1900s was a hotbed of intellectualism and the birthplace of modern design. The Wiener Werkstatte (Vienna Workshop) was formed in 1903, and produced a vast range of goods in a bold, modern, geometric style. These designs, in turn, were to prove hugely influential to the next generation of architects and designers of the Bauhaus and Modern movement in the 1920s.

Collection of vases designed by Keith Murray for Wedgwood. The 11 in shouldered vase on the right was first advertised 1934 for 18s 6d (83p). By 2000 its value had risen to approximately £1,000

BRAVE NEW WORLD

The influential 1925 *Exposition Internationale des Arts Decoratifs* in Paris spawned Art Deco, and inspired struggling architect Keith Murray to move into glass and ceramic design. In 1933, he began a fruitful association with Wedgwood, where he developed machine-turned, minimalist forms in a range of subtle colours. An eleven-inch shouldered vase, designed by Murray for Wedgwood, was advertised in 1934 for eighteen shillings and sixpence (83p). By 2000, its value had risen to about £1,000.

An invitation by Mappin & Webb to design a range of modern silver for the 1935 Exhibition of British Art in Industry marked the pinnacle of Murray's design career. After 1945, he concentrated on architecture, but his designs remained in production into the 1950s. Examples of his glassware for Stevens & Williams can generally be bought for £400 to £600, although larger vases have made over £1,000.

THE CHROME AGE

Technological advances made in plastics, tubular steel, chromium plating and bent plywood construction during and after the First World War meant designers could produce exciting, affordable goods for the mass market.

If one material defined the twentieth century, it is chrome. First used as a coating for missiles during the war, chrome became available commercially in 1925. It was used to plate much of the tubular steel furniture and lighting of the modernists in the 1920s and 1930s, and has since been used extensively in design. A chrome-plated dining chair, designed by Harry Bertoia for Knoll Associates in about 1950, would now cost between £120 and £150.

LESS IS MORE

With vast areas of Finland covered in birch forest, architect Alvar Aalto didn't have far to look when deciding on a material for his furniture. Following an exhibition of his work at Fortnum & Mason's in 1933, Aalto's designs for bent ply furniture were well received by the British, who preferred its soft, curvilinear forms to the hard-edged modernism of tubular steel favoured on the continent. Aalto's furniture has survived in large quantities and smaller pieces are still affordable. Most common is the small, circular topped stool. The laminated birch tops were available unstained, ebonised and in a variety of colours, all bearing the Finmar ivorene label pinned to the underside. They can generally be bought now for £200.

The great unsung hero of British design, in my opinion, is the innovative Gerald Summers, who gave up engineering to form Makers of Simple Furniture with his wife in 1931. Their furniture exploited the flexible qualities of aeroplane ply, first developed in glider construction during the First World War. His greatest achievement was his one-piece bent ply armchair of 1934, an icon of modern design which surpassed anything else at the time. Summers succeeded in creating a single fluid form from a sheet of ply, eliminating the need of a supporting frame. Reputedly, only 120 were produced, retailing in 1935 for three pounds and fifteen shillings (£3.75). If you could find one today, it would be worth about £20,000.

Chrome wire dining chair, designed by Harry Bertoia for Knoll Associates circa 1950. Now costs £120 – £150

THE NEW LOOK

No period witnessed more change than the post-war to 1960s era, which saw the birth of teenage culture and fashion, rock and roll and the space age. Due to post-war austerity, many pre-war commercial designs were produced well into the 1950s. Shortages of raw materials introduced economic utility furniture, and rationing and restrictions.

In 1947, Christian Dior shook the fashion world with his New Look collection. It also influenced furniture and ceramics, which were shaking off the post-war blues in exciting, colourful, organic shapes and patterns inspired by Joan Miro and Jackson Pollock. Examples include ranges designed for Midwinter by Terence Conran and by Jessie

Bent ply armchair, designed by Gerald Summers, 1934, retailing in 1935 for £3.75. Now worth about £20,000

Tait, and free-form pottery by Poole.

In 1950s Britain, Robin and Lucienne Day were the designer couple, much as Charles and Ray Eames had been in America. Robin is perhaps best known for his polypropylene chair, one of the most commercially successful pieces of furniture ever produced. Since 1963, over 14 million have been sold worldwide. They were used in classrooms throughout the country. In 2000, Tom Dixon, Habitat's director of design, launched the 20th Century Legend Collection, which included a reissue of Day's chair. This was made available to a new generation in an exciting range of translucent colours.

Lucienne Day is best known as a textile designer, and her 'Calyx' design for the Festival of Britain in 1951 brought her international recognition. She continued to design for Heal's up to the 1970s, extending into wallpaper and carpet design. Her early textiles are in great demand and can be difficult to find. Lengths are likely to cost from £100 to £400.

White ABS plastic umbrella stand, designed by Giancarlo Piretti for Castelli, 1969; rug, designed by Pierre Cardin Studio, circa 1970

ONE SMALL STEP

In the 1960s and 70s, designers had a wish either to blow up or knock down. Furniture was inflatable, disposable and collapsible, as, after Pop Art, designers began to oppose classic notions of good taste.

Surprisingly, the space age had far more influence on European designers than on their American counterparts, bringing about a radical view of future living styles. Italian designer Joe Colombo's work captures the mood of this time. He envisaged the break-up of traditional family units into a highly evolved tribal society, requiring a new type of habitat. His innovative designs have

one recurring theme: multi-functioning capacity. No design demonstrates this better than his 'Tube' chair of 1969, consisting of four padded plastic cylinders of varying diameters, which can be clipped together to create a series of sofas, chairs and stools. When not in use, all components fit inside each other. Early examples now cost from £6,000 to £8,000, but one in good condition, and still in its original bag, would probably be worth a third more.

The majority of Colombo's designs are no longer in production, and, while many items of furniture and lighting sell for several thousands of pounds, it is still possible to purchase a small plastic 'Boby' trolley for approximately £200 to £300.

LESS IS A BORE

French designer Philippe Starck is undeniably the only true international design star of the new millennium. He has produced designs for furniture, interiors, lighting and domestic appliances, continuing the long tradition of stylish French design. Trained as a furniture designer, Starck was appointed artistic director at Pierre Cardin and, during the 1970s, was noted for his startling Parisian nightclub interiors. In 1983, he was commissioned to design furniture for President Mitterrand's private apartment at the Elysée Palace, to great critical acclaim.

Like the great architect-designers of a century before, Starck has complete control over his interiors. In 1988, he finished the first of many hotel interiors, designing everything down to the bath taps. In the 1990s he designed toothbrushes, door handles and a lemon squeezer for Alessi, which no chic 1990s kitchen would be complete

'Calyx' textile design by Lucienne Day for Heals, exhibited at the Festival of Britain, 1951

Resources

Further reading

Christopher Dresser, 1834–1904, Michael Whiteway, Skira, 2001

Robin & Lucienne Day, Lesley Jackson, Mitchell Beazley, 2001

20th Century Ceramic Designers, Andrew Casey, Antique Collectors'
  Club, 2001

The Dream Factory: Alessi since 1921, Alberto Alessi, Electra, 2003

Joe Colombo and Italian Design of the Sixties, Ignazia Favata, Thames
  & Hudson, 1988

Decorative Arts: 1850–1950, British Museum Catalogue, 1991

Century of Design, Penny Sparke, Mitchell Beazley, 1998

Miller's Buyers' Guide, Miller's Publications, 2003

Wat is Art Nouveau en Art Deco Waard, 2 volumes, Uitgeverit Scriptum
  Art, Holland, 2003

Modern design sale catalogues produced by the big three auction
houses (Sotheby's, Christie's and Bonhams) are a good source
of information for dealers and collectors alike.

Museums

Brighton Museum & Art Gallery (Art Nouveau and Art Deco)
T: 01273 290900 www.brighton.virtualmuseum.info

Design Museum (twentieth-century product design), London SE1
T: 0870 909 9009 www.designmuseum.org

Hunterian Museum and Art Gallery (Mackintosh furniture
and designs), University of Glasgow
T: 0141 330 4221 (museum) T: 0141 330 5431 (art gallery)
www.hunterian.gla.ac.uk

Specialist dealers and internet sites

20th Century Marks, Kent T: 01959 562221
www.20thcenturymarks.co.uk

Le Style 25, London T: 020 8983 4285
www.lestyle25.com

Imagebank, Derby T: 07711 030493
www.imagebank.uk.com

James Strang, St Andrews, Fife T: 07950 490088
www.mod-i.com

Bent Ply, London T: 020 7724 2544
www.bentply.com

The Country Seat, Henley-on-Thames, Oxon
T: 01491 64149 www.thecountryseat.com

without. The latter is still available for about £40.
In 2000, Alessi brought out a gold-plated, limited
edition version to mark its tenth anniversary.

Italian firm Alessi was founded as a plating
workshop and foundry in 1921 by Giovanni Alessi
Anghini. In 1983, they celebrated the launch of
their Officina Alessi range by inviting eleven
leading architects and designers, including
Michael Graves, Alessandro Mendini and Robert
Venturi, to design tea and coffee sets. The results
were witty and colourful, and very collectable.
Each set was produced in Continental 925 silver,
and the production run was limited to 99. These
sets now cost between £6,400 and £32,000,
depending on the designer.

Red/Blue Chair, circa 1923, designed by Gerrit Thomas Rietveld, 1888–1964. Now worth as much as £300,000

TIMELINE

Somewhat ironically, Dutch architect Gerrit Rietveld's now famous Red/Blue chair did not start life either red or blue! It was originally made of dark stained oak. It was not until Rietveld allied himself to the De Stijl (The Style) movement that the first painted version, using the primary colours of Piet Mondrian painting, emerged around 1923. The early, unpainted version from 1918 now sells for around £120,000, but the later, painted version from 1923 is more valuable. It had a black stained wooden frame, a plywood back and seat lacquered red and blue, with terminals in yellow. Made by Rietveld's assistant, Gerard van de Groenekan of Utrecht, these painted chairs are extremely rare. Costing about £6 when they were made in 1923, they would have been selling for £350 to £500 in 1950. Now an original edition could be worth as much as £300,000. Editions made by Cassina of Italy from the 1970s can be bought for £1,000 to £1,500.

CRYSTAL BALL

Alessi's widely available design-led products of the 1980s and 1990s will become future collectables. Production is grouped under three trademarks: Alessi, for stainless steel and plastic; Officina Alessi, for small limited production pieces by specific designers in silver and other materials; and Tendentse, for porcelain. In 1993, Alessi introduced a conical bowl, 'Christy', moulded in thermoplastic and available in a wide range of colours. From an 1885 design by Dr Christopher Dresser, it was promoted as an item of 'modern' design and has proved to be very successful. The doctor would have approved!

A selection of items from Alessi: Michael Grave's 'Singing Kettle', 1992; Christopher Dresser 'Christy' conical bowl, 1993; Alessandro Mendini's 'Anna G' corkscrew, 1994

10

DANIEL AGNEW ON
TOYS AND DOLLS

TIM WONNACOTT

"You don't get a much better expert than a chap who started as a porter in the auction business and, by dint of fifteen years' hard work, rises to become head of department at a firm like Christie's. Daniel has seen thousands of toys come and go and several fortunes made in the process! "

TEDDY BEARS

The most successful twentieth-century toy is the teddy bear. In 1902, after visiting a circus, Richard Steiff realised life-like movement was missing from his soft toys. He produced a group of jointed animals, which included a bear, for the 1903 Leipzig Spring Trade Fair. They soon took off and, during 1907, Steiff alone sold one million bears.

In the 1910s and 1920s, many new companies started making teddy bears, and established toy manufacturers, like Bing and Schuco in Germany, also changed to bears. Major British companies, like Dean's Rag Book, joined the bandwagon, as did Chad Valley, Farnell, Chiltern and Merrythought.

The teddy bear's appeal waned during the 1960s and 1970s because of man-made synthetic plushes and cheap Far Eastern imports. But the story comes full circle. Antique teddy bears' renewed popularity has spurred traditional companies still in business to make traditional teddy bears again.

During the 1980s, the price of antique teddy bears soared. In 1989, a rare red Steiff teddy bear called Alfonzo sold for a staggering £12,650, three times the then world record price for a teddy bear. Since the early 1990s, it is fairly standard for a bear to sell for over £30,000 and the world record for an antique teddy bear is £110,000. However, you can still buy old teddy bears for under £100.

A selection of teddy bears. Estimates range from £1,000 – £6,000, all Steiff, 1905–1930s. The large golden bear is by J.K. Farnell

DOLLS

The major manufacturers of what were mainly bisque-headed (unglazed porcelain) dolls during the early twentieth century were German companies such as Armand Marseille, Simon & Halbig and Ernst Heubach. The rare mould numbers that command higher prices nowadays came from the less prolific manufacturers, including Kestner and Kämmer & Reinhardt. All manufacturers made standard 'dolly-faced' dolls, with open/closing eyes and an open mouth. But it is the unusual mould numbered dolls with sad faces and closed, pouty mouths that reach record prices – sometimes over £20,000.

Generally, during the 1920s and 1930s, composition took over from bisque as the main manufactured material. Germany still led the field, but, after the Second World War, Britain began to manufacture more for the home market.

The real revolution came in 1959 with Barbie. Ruth and Elliot Handler discovered a Bild Lilli doll made after a risqué Hamburg cartoon strip of the same name. Their toy manufacturing company turned this into the very successful Barbie, named after their daughter, Barbara. A boxed No 1 Barbie from this period can now sell for over £3,000.

VEHICLES

Motorised transportation has been key in toys. Early cars, boats and aircraft were originally depicted in tin plate and hand-painted. As time moved on lithographed decoration was developed. Initially, they were steam-powered but key-wind clockwork mechanisms quickly took over.

Germany again led, although smaller manufacturers in France, the United Kingdom and America were also involved. The Rolls Royce of tinplate manufacture was Märklin, which produced expensive, quality toys, which have a premium now. Other German companies included Bing, Güntherman, Schuco and Lehmann. Although they continued to be manufactured into the 1960s, their popularity was overtaken by Japanese toys.

A British initiative was the diecast smaller scale vehicle, developed to go with 'o' gauge toy railway systems. The popularity of Hornby Trains meant that children wanted all sorts of accessories. So, in 1924, Meccano, the parent company of Hornby, developed six 'Modelled Miniatures', which now sell for between £500 and £1,500, depending on colour.

These Dinky Toys became one of the biggest successes of the 1950s and 1960s. Every type of vehicle was produced. Dinky had competitors like Spot On, Lesney Matchbox, who made a smaller scale car, and Corgi, who became more successful than Dinky in the 1970s with their TV and film related ranges. A early, gold-coloured James Bond car, in mint condition, is now worth around £200.

From left to right – A Distler clockwork six-light Limousine, circa 1930, £300 – £400; a Carette clockwork four-seat
Open Tourer, circa 1912, £1,000 – £1,200, and a Schuco battery-operated Mercedes 190SL, circa 1957, £100 – £200

Pre-war Dinky Toys – 1933–1940, £100 – £1,000 each

For diecast collectors, condition is vital. They have to be mint and in their original box. But colour makes the biggest difference. Most vehicles were painted in one or two set colour variants. But, occasionally, a car would be given an odd colour finish, which can sometimes make it worth four to ten times the value of the standard car. For instance, a Dinky 159 Morris Oxford, with a dark green body and dark green hubs, sells for between £100 and £120. The same model, with a blue body and grey hubs, will be worth £1,500.

TRAINS

Märklin, along with Bing, dominated toy trains from the early 1900s, adapting their range to match the trains of the countries they produced for.

After the First World War, toy buyers became nationalistic and sales of German products decreased. During the 1920s Frank Hornby developed his 'o' gauge range, which his company went on to export all over the world.

Economies recovered slowly after 1945, and Hornby's Dublo ('oo') range, developed just prior to World War Two, came into its own. This smaller, more economic system became a favourite with boys everywhere through the 1940s to the 1960s.

Most British trains were painted in the great pre-Nationalisation livery. Great names like Great Western Railway (GWR), London North Eastern Railways (LNER), Southern Railway (SR) and all the famous locomotives, including 'Sir Nigel Gresley', 'Princess Elizabeth' and 'Flying Scotsman' were represented.

Their values vary greatly. Most companies made a starter set, either a goods set or passenger set, which are generally quite common. If you caught the train bug as a child and went on to collect further locomotives and accessories, you will probably have found the rarer and more valuable items. A Hornby Dublo train set may cost as little as £40–£50 but, at the other end of the spectrum, is a Märklin Gauge V train, sold in 2002 for a record-breaking £113,750.

Left to right – An 'O' gauge Carette for Bassett-Lowke clockwork GNR Atlantic Locomotive and Tender 4-4-2 No 235, circa 1908, £3,000 – £4,000; an 'O' gauge Märklin electric Flying Hamburger two-car Diesel Articulated Unit, circa 1937, £700 – £1,000; an 'O' Hornby Series clockwork Lord Nelson locomotive and tender, circa 1934, £300 – £400; and a 'OO' pre-war Märklin HR700 LMS 4-6-2 locomotive and tender, 1937-38, £1,500 – £2,000

Left to right – Heyde mounted band of the Life Guards, set of 12, circa 1910, £400–£500; various Britains highlanders, 1920–1930s, £10–£15 each; and items from Britains Home Farm series, £2–£10 each

HOLLOW-CAST SOLDIERS AND FIGURES

In 1893 William Britain revolutionised the production of toy soldiers when he invented a method of making hollow lead soldiers by spinning the mould so the lead just stuck to its outside. The lower production costs made toy soldiers more affordable.

These 54-millimetre-high soldiers represented all types of military uniforms. The popular range was British ceremonial figures depicting the Coronations, Trooping the Colour or other state occasions. During both World Wars, the khaki troops of the British army, and all their vehicles and guns, were depicted in the range.

After the First World War, the country was in a pro-disarmament mood, so Britains added civilian figures. Their Home Farm items were the most popular and included a Village Idiot after a passing remark by Queen Mary at the 1927 British Industries Fair. The most common pink or beige-smocked Village Idiots now sell at £100 to £200; the less common ones, in two different shades of green, may make between £400 and £500.

Toy soldier production restarted slowly after the Second World War. With restrictions on lead use in the home market, Britains began exporting, creating new sets sold as 'Regiments of all Nations'. The Coronation of Queen Elizabeth II also boosted the market, and the sale of Coronation Coaches was a big part of Britains' business.

During the 1950s, plastic figures became popular and were promoted as unbreakable. In 1965, after a law banned use of lead in toys, Britains converted their entire range to plastic. Britains, one of England's oldest toy companies, is still going strong.

SPACE TOYS AND ROBOTS

The 1930s and 1940s marked an increased interest in science fiction. In 1956, a Hollywood B movie, *Forbidden Planet*, featured a robot called Robby, with space travel beginning the following year with the first Sputnik satellite. A few early robots were produced in the 1940s, but, during the late 1950s and early 1960s, all manner of flashing, walking, talking and firing robots and spacecraft were produced. Initially, the robots were clockwork but soon battery-operated versions became more popular and more complex.

Early tin plate toy robots are highly collectable. Plastic productions of the late 1960s and 1970s have little more than decorative value. More common robots can still be bought for around £100, but, a few years ago, a Masudaya Machine Man robot, made in Japan in the late 1950s, sold for £29,900.

DISNEY, TV AND FILM

Film and television have recently been the major influence on toy production. Early film-makers were quick to market related merchandise. Leading characters such as Charlie Chaplin's Tramp, Shirley Temple, Felix the Cat and Mickey Mouse are some of the more obvious commercially successful characters. All manner of related merchandise was produced, ranging from dolls, clockwork toys, board games to children's tea sets. Early 1930s Disney toys can be highly desirable.

Characters made famous by radio's *Listen With Mother* and, later, *Watch With Mother* also became very popular as toys. Moko's Muffin the Mule metal puppet, in its original box, will now make £300 to £400. But other characters, including Andy Pandy, Bill and Ben and Noddy, were also represented.

The 1960s and 1970s saw a real boom. James Bond's Aston Martin DB5 was one of the biggest selling toys ever. Other action characters had their vehicles brought to life by Dinky and Corgi – Thunderbirds 2 and 4, Lady Penelope's pink Rolls Royce, the Batmobile, the Starsky and Hutch Ford Grand Torino, for instance.

Television greats such as Basil Brush, Parsley the Lion and *The Magic Roundabout* inspired toy ranges for younger children. Corgi made a whole *Magic Roundabout* playground with a roundabout, train and characters like Dougal and Zeebedee. A very expensive item at the time, it sold in limited numbers. Now this model in perfect boxed condition can be worth as much as £800.

TOYS OF RECENT MANUFACTURE

Film and television promotional toys seem to be the most collected areas. The most obvious area is *Star Wars* toys, which have been produced in vast quantities. Consequently, *Star Wars* collectors would only want them in perfect boxed condition and, ideally, the individual figures in unopened packaging. Recently, some of the early figures, made by Palitoy rather than the usual Kenner, sold for between £300 and £1,000 each. These were all mint in their original blister packs. But this is very much the exception to the rule. Most played-with figures are worth only a few pounds each.

Today, many people have become aware of the value of old toys and so many new ones are being kept mint or mint and boxed. These are not being used for their original purpose, which is for children to play with.

Various robots including a rare Nomura Robby Space Patrol, late 1950s, £2,000–£4,000

Left to right – a Moko Muffin Junior puppet, £200–£300; a Dean's Rag Book Mickey Mouse, £80–£100; a Corgi Junior Batman set, late 1970s, £150–£200 and a Corgi James Bond Aston Martin DB5, in rare blister pack, £200–£300

Left to right – A McDonald's Animal, 2002; a 'light-up' Pink Panther made for KFC, 2001; a Kellogg's Darth Maul from Star Wars Episode I; a Peyo King Smurf; and an original Luke Skywalker. (The Smurf and Luke are from my childhood toy box and the others were gathered from various hamburger-loving colleagues)

Resources

Further Reading

Dolls, Olivia Bristol, DeAgostini Editions, 1997

Christie's Toy Railways, Hugo Marsh, Pavilion Books Ltd, 2002

Wheels: Christie's Presents the Magical World of Automotive Toys, Mike and Sue Richardson, Chronicle Books, 1999

The Great Book of Hollow-cast Figures, Norman Joplin, New Cavendish Books, 1993

A Collector's Guide to Bears, Sue Pearson, Mitchell Beazley, 2001

Price Guides

Ramsay's British Diecast Model Toys Catalogue, Swapmeet Publications

Blue Book Dolls and Values, Jan Foulke, Hobby House Press Inc

Opie's Pocket Price Guide to Britains Hollowcast Toy Soldiers, New Cavendish Books

Internet Sites

Teddy Bears

www.oldbear.co.uk

www.sue-pearson.co.uk

Museums

Bethnal Green Museum of Childhood, London E2

T: 020 8980 2415   www.vam.ac.uk/vastatic/nmc

The Brighton Toy and Model Museum, Brighton, East Sussex

T: 01273 749494   www.brightontoymuseum.co.uk

Puppenhaus Museum, Basel, Switzerland

T: 00 41 61 225 9595   www.puppenhausmuseum.ch

A very rare Steiff Hot-water bottle teddy bear with original metal canister, circa 1907. One of only ninety examples made between 1907 and 1914.

TIMELINE

Steiff teddy bears have been popular with children for almost a century. Interest in them as collectables is, however, more recent, and it is only in the last twenty or so years that their value has really begun to rocket, as can be seen from this timeline for a rare Steiff hot water bottle teddy bear

1907 – £2
1910 to 1960 – no collectable value
1970 – £200
1980 – £1,000
1990 – £10,000
2000 – £30,000

A selection of Harry Potter film and book merchandise currently available including a figure of Ginny Weasley by Mattel and a Rubik's Magic Harry Potter puzzle.

CRYSTAL BALL

Anything television or film related seems to be the strongest field for a future collectable. A strong contender at present is likely to be the merchandise from the Harry Potter books and films, especially the early batches of toys. Bear in mind, of course, that their condition will be crucial. Anything in perfect condition and in its original packaging will be worth far more – particularly for something like Harry Potter, which has been so staggeringly popular.

11

HENRY SANDON ON
POTTERY AND PORCELAIN

TIM WONNACOTT

They say that enthusiasm is infectious, and I don't know a more infectious enthusiast than Henry. I challenge anyone with only a passing interest in ceramics to sit with Henry for twenty minutes and not come away feeling potty about pots! Genial, extremely knowledgeable and unselfishly keen to impart what he knows, he really is a lovely man both on and off the screen.

Science was my most hated lesson at school. In consequence, I remember little of the subject except for two statements: 'Things that go up must come down' and 'Perpetual motion is impossible'.

How do these theories apply to twentieth-century ceramics? Do prices always go up or do they go down as well? Is there any perpetuity in collecting or factories? Let me give a couple of examples from Royal Worcester, of which I was curator for many years.

ROYAL WORCESTER

In the 1960s the great Royal Worcester artist Harry Davis, then in his eighties and still painting, asked me to find out the price of one of his vases in Bygones antiques shop near the factory. It stood in the window, a magnificent sixteen-inch high vase painted by Harry in 1908 with one of his superb studies of Highland sheep in a misty Scottish setting. The factory price of the vase in 1908 would have been about one and a half guineas.

'It's not bad,' said Harry, in his self-deprecating way. While Harry hid, I boldly asked the owner, Docherty Bullock. 'For you,' said Docherty, chewing things over, '£28'. I thanked him and returned to a nervous Harry. Although he didn't have any of his own sheep paintings, he grumbled that he couldn't afford it, hurried back to the factory and never bought the vase.

After he died, his work became very collectable and prices have risen because such things are works of art; a much smaller vase with Harry's sheep painting was sold at Bonhams in 2000 for £6,600. A large plaque would make at least £8,000 to £10,000, being rarer and more highly regarded. This may seem high but this is a one-off item by the greatest twentieth-century British ceramic artist. The cost of a new bone china plaque, made by the present day leading manufacturer – Bronté Porcelain Company – and painted by a painter such as Milwyn Holloway, a pupil of Harry Davis, would be £2,000 for a 23 x 17 in, and £5,500 for a 38 x 27 in example. This takes into account the superb quality and difficulty of manufacture.

Not everything behaves so explosively. Fine large birds and animals made by Royal Worcester from the 1950s to the 1980s, some originally costing thousands of pounds, can often now be bought at auction for a fraction of their cost price. This applies to other companies, such as Boehm, and the values can be dispiriting. There are exceptions, such as Doris Lindner's great models of the Arab Stallion, Princess Elizabeth on Tommy, or Arkle, which have kept up with inflation. The superb bird models of Dorothy Doughty have also slumped in price. Perhaps now is the time to buy if you like them.

The incredible reticulated wares of George Owen are another type of Worcester porcelain that has zoomed upwards, like the vases and plaques of Davis, the Stintons, Hawkins and Sebright. These magical pieces, which cost a pound or two between 1900 and 1916, were running at £100 or so in the 1950s. They went

Royal Worcester, *Princess Elizabeth on Tommy*, by Doris Lindner, dating from 1949. Sold at Bonhams in 2003 for £2,900.

up quickly in the 1980s and, by 2000, sizable perfect pieces were reaching high thousands, exceptional ones £10,000 to £20,000. One little high heeled shoe, in its original 1910 box, and marked with the price of one pound ten shillings (£1.50), was sold for £4,000 in the 1990s.

ROYAL DOULTON

Royal Doulton has also seen interesting price changes. There are two factories to consider: the original one in Lambeth, which mainly made saltglaze stoneware, and the other, in Burslem in the Potteries, which made earthenware and bone china. Henry Doulton encouraged the talented Lambeth factory girls to personalise their work

Royal Worcester covered bowl by George Owen, made in 1921. Sold at Bonhams in 2002 for £10,000

Pair of Royal Doulton vases by Hannah Barlow. Sold at Bonhams in 2003 for £1,500 the pair

with special marks, and these variations are part of the fun of ownership. Prices have moved upwards with the publication of *The Doulton Lambeth Wares* by Desmond Eyles, which has listed all the marks and illustrated large numbers of their works.

It always surprised me how little these pieces sold for some years ago, compared with the higher prices for Doulton Burslem character jugs and figures, but things are changing. Worth looking out for are the incredible scraffito animals by Hannah Barlow, with vigorous dogs, horses and lions, forming a complete landscape around the vessels. A wonderful pair of large vases turned up at a Dorset *Antiques Roadshow*. Possibly made for the Australian market, they had kangaroos hopping all around, and were worth £8,000 to £10,000.

Other collectable Lambeth artists are Harry Simeon, Mark Marshall, Eliza Simmance, Frank Butler and Florence Barlow. My own favourite is the modeller, George Tinworth, whose work ranged from detailed biblical plaques to humorous studies of mice and frogs. Coming up at auction as I write is a group depicting a pair of mice musicians playing a harp and a squeezebox, fronting a menu holder which is broken. Even so, the fun of the piece produces an estimate of £800 to £1,200. Look out for the mice watching a Punch and Judy show or going to the Derby.

Doulton Burslem character jugs and figures comprise a huge collecting field, with prices governed by rarity (the shorter the run the higher the value). Some pieces were issued in different, rare colourways and you need to know whether a clown, say, has red hair or not, as the value can vary enormously, from a few hundred to a few thousand pounds.

A group of Beswick horses, dating from 1950s to 1970s. Sold at Bonhams in 2003 for between £200 and £450

Books have revolutionised the collecting of twentieth-century ceramics. Remember, however, that prices at auction vary greatly and the pieces themselves also vary in quality and condition. Collectors' clubs give guidance, hold swap meets, and gather like-minded collectors together. These clubs deal mostly with factories whose history does not cover the whole of the twentieth century, such as Beswick, so we can only track their progress through the second half. Many Beswick wares have shown incredible rises, their horse and bull models fetching as much as the better modelled and decorated models of Doris Lindner for Royal Worcester. Some of these make from £500 to £1,000.

OTHER MAJOR COMPANIES

Manufacturers throughout the century include Wedgwood, Spode, Coalport, Derby and Minton (now no more, although the Minton name is being continued by Doulton). Minton produced magnificent work, such as their nineteenth-century majolica ware, which has long been collected, especially by Americans. A life-sized model of a peacock fetched an incredible £100,000 at a recent auction. The great designer John Wadsworth produced some fascinating Art Nouveau style pieces in the early 1900s, which would repay keen collecting. Even the *pâte-sur-pâte* decorated pieces by Alboin Birks have not yet reached what they should, considering the work involved.

Vase by Désiré Leroy for Royal Crown Derby, dating from 1897. Sold at Bonhams in 2001, with the cover lacking, for £4,200. With its lid, it would be worth £12,000

depicting elves and fairies, bought originally for a few pounds, can now fetch £5,000 to £10,000. A magnificent piece, decorated with 'The Ghostly Wood' pattern, was brought into an *Antiques Roadshow*. The magnificent, creepy design, depicting a white rabbit running away from frightening ghosts and ghoulies, scared its owner as a girl. Now she is much happier with it, valued at £10,000 and rising.

Around 1930, the rage for Art Deco was exemplified by the work of Clarice Cliff, who taught the girls at Wilkinson's pottery to paint colourful patterns in the Bizarre and other patterns. The simple stock patterns of the 1930s and 1940s by Clarice Cliff have gone down in value. They cost very little when they came out, but cheered people up after the post-war depression years. For years, they languished in cupboards, regarded as vulgar and cheap, then suddenly became all the rage. Values had risen by 2000, especially for rare versions which can fetch many hundreds per piece.

There were two other great designers in Stoke-on-Trent in the 1920s and 1930s: Charlotte Rhead and Susie Cooper. Susie's work has not increased greatly, but one of Charlotte's Burleigh Ware (Burgess and Leigh) plaques has just sold for £2,900. This was not too far removed from the wonderful, highly collectable Moorcroft factory tube-lined pieces.

Spode produced some fine wares in the twentieth century and later merged with Royal Worcester. Many mergers have taken place in the British ceramic industry: Coalport merged with Wedgwood but their best work was produced when they were a separate company from 1900 to the 1920s. The paintings of such fine painters as Ball and Chivers are now collectable and will

Royal Crown Derby's equivalent great work was by Désiré Leroy, who painted flowers in the French style. His application of superb gilding has caused his work to follow the spectacular rise of that George Owen at Royal Worcester. £18,000 is not unexpected for a fine piece and may rise.

By the late twentieth century, the Derby factory was part of a large group but a buy-out now finds them on their own again. A reinvigorated company, they are producing highly collectable, stylised animal models decorated with the traditional Imari patterns.

The Wedgwood Company's most exciting and collectable twentieth-century wares were designed in the 1920s by Daisy Makeig-Jones, with fairyland decorations. Larger vases or plaques become more so. Many other companies such as Shelley and Ruskin produced their best work in that period and should be looked at.

SMALL COMPANIES AND INDIVIDUAL POTTERS

Many small studio potteries had just one or two potters making individual pieces. Chief among the earliest ones were the Martin Brothers of London, who created imaginative stoneware vases and figures. The most exciting were their bird-headed pots, all different and humorous. Prices have gone from £10 in the 1920s to £100 in 1950 to several thousand today. The great Edwin Beer Fishley (1861–1902), of Fremington in Devon, produced gorgeous incised and slip decorated jugs that had a big influence on Bernard Leach, the father of modern craft pottery. Leech established his pottery in St Ives in Cornwall in 1921, and his pots and tiles are among the most collectable twentieth-century pieces, costing only a few pounds when first made, rising to £50 when exhibited in galleries in the 1950s. Prices now run into the low thousands.

Seek out modern potters, visit their potteries and look at their work in exhibitions or in the craft potters' shop in Soho, London. See if you can pick a potter whose work is going to be as collectable as Hans Coper and Dame Lucie Rie. They came to London from Austria before the war and together produced the most exciting pots of the century. It is still possible to find fine examples of their work in specialised auctions at prices ranging from a few hundred pounds for simple pieces by Rie up to many thousands for some of the monumental pieces by Coper.

At a recent contemporary ceramics auction at Bonhams in London you could have acquired a Rie porcelain small vase with flaring rim for £500 or a large stoneware vase inlaid with bands of blue and radiating lines for £7,500; or an early planter by Coper, circa 1950, for £800, ranging up to £23,000 for a ten and a half inch high sack form with disc top, circa 1972. These could have been bought for a fraction of these prices before the potters became famous and died. Buy a pot you like from the potter himself, for the money you could spend on a meal. The meal will be gone within 24 hours but the pot will be your friend forever.

Thistle-form vase by Hans Coper, dating from circa 1975. Sold at Bonhams in 2002 for £18,000

Resources

Further reading

Royal Worcester Porcelain: From 1862 to the Present Day, Henry Sandon, Barrie & Jenkins, 1979

Starting to Collect Antique Porcelain, John Sandon, Antique Collectors Club, 2003

Miller's Guide to Collecting Porcelain, John Sandon, Miller's Publications, 2002

The Doulton Lambeth Wares, Desmond Eyles, Richard Dennis Publications, 2002

Price Guides

Antiques Price Guide, Judith Miller, Miller's Publications

Exhibitions

There are monthly exhibitions of new work at **Contemporary Ceramics**, London W1 T:020 7437 7605

Museums

Potteries Museum, Stoke on Trent T: 01782 232323
www.2002.stoke.gov.uk/museums

Museum of Worcester Porcelain, Worcester
T: 01905 746000 www.royal-worcester.co.uk

TIMELINE

Work by Harry Davis is now highly collectable. One of his vases, painted with a superb study of Highland sheep, would have cost the equivalent of £1.60 or so in 1908, £28 in 1967, £1,000 in 1980, £4,000 in the year 2000 (when it was sold in a sale at Bonhams). The price is still going up.

Royal Worcester sheep-decorated vase by Harry Davis, dating from 1913. Sold at Bonhams in 2000 for £6,600

Scraffito fish paste pot and cover by Julia Carter Preston sold at the Walker Art Gallery exhibition in 2000 for £75

CRYSTAL BALL

Who is the Lucie Rie for the 21st century? Might it be Julia Carter Preston, an incredibly talented potter working in the Bluecoat Chambers in Liverpool? Her retrospective in 2000 at the Walker Art Gallery was a sellout. Pictured here is a classic scraffito fish paste pot and cover, with typical Carter Preston iridescent glaze and charming sardine finial. It could have been yours for £75.

12

ADAM HILLS ON ARCHITECTURAL COLLECTABLES

Adam Hills, a young reclamation entrepreneur, spots objects and trends in terms of retrievable décor, which older people (like me!) miss because we often scrapped the now desirable object twenty years ago! I remember only too well the English Rose sink unit I threw out in 1988 and Adam now says that this was definitely not the thing to have done!

TIM WONNACOTT

Although I have a degree in architecture, I really learned about buildings when I started rummaging in skips while renovating my first flat. Like many other dealers and designers before me, inspiration and profit came from *objets trouvés*. In scrap, reclamation, or architectural antiques – call them what you will – there is an element of serendipity that is pleasing to the heart, and ecological reuse that is good for the brain, wallet and environment. Through salvage one can learn how a building comes apart and so how it can go back together. Even now I cannot pass a skip without having a look at what's in it – and it's well worth it if you have even a passing interest in collecting for your home, or acquiring unusual items which might appreciate in future.

Architectural antiques include items from eighteenth-century marble fireplaces, like the one pictured worth about £20,000, down to bricks and cast iron baths. The origins of architectural reuse are centuries old, with examples of Roman bricks and columns being used in medieval churches, and panelled rooms relocated between country houses. Only in the last century have disposable consumer products broken earlier habits, but the

A George III statuary marble chimney piece valued at £20,000.
The pure miky white marble is Italian but the style is very English

The economic depression and social change of the inter-war years saw the break-up of hundreds of country estates and stately houses. Vast piles across Britain were knocked down, while others were stripped out for use as schools and hospitals. Dispersal sales often sold off the panelling, chimney pieces, carvings and ornaments cheaply, although much also was destroyed.

In the post-war years, the demolition continued, with slum clearances, urban restructuring, and motorways carving through town and country. As war damage was repaired, the country turned slowly from austerity to affluence. But some saw the value in the Georgian and Victorian terraces that yielded to the sledgehammer. Alongside the conservation lobby and amenity societies like the National Trust, the Society for the Protection of Ancient Buildings (SPAB), the Georgian Group and the Victorian Society, came a new generation of salvage dealer. Over the last 30 years or so, the domestic market has been stimulated by public interest in period buildings.

The salvage dealer ignores nothing – from floors to doors, bathroom and kitchen fittings, fireplaces, windows, in all styles and dates. As Georgian fittings became more appreciated, prices escalated and their rarity increased. The market moved on, so most dealers' stock-in-trade became Victorian fittings, such as cast iron baths and fireplaces, feature beams and bricks. Now fashion has progressed beyond the stripped pine Victoriana so popular in the 1980s, Edwardian, Deco, Utility and Retro are coming into their own.

It is not, however, a conventionally collectable area. Because of their size and weight, most architectural antiques cannot be kept in a cabinet,

green lobby is keen for us to relearn them. Reclamation makes ecological sense and is also bound up with the preservation of our recent design past, and with the increasingly valuable field of antiques.

It's not easy to make money from architectural antiques unless you're a salvage expert or a serious dealer. But you can make good buys for your own home, which may well add to its value in the long term.

although there are museums and collections where they are displayed. The Brooking Collection, at the University of Greenwich, is a fascinating accumulation of timber mouldings, sash windows, doors and fire grates. Many other collections, such as the Geffrye Museum, the Victoria and Albert Museum and the Burrell Collection in Glasgow, display panelled rooms, chimney pieces, door cases and other valuable carvings. High profile exhibitions stimulate the market for the style, designer, material or area featured. A recent Imperial War Museum exhibition of Eric Ravilious's work had a marked effect: a Wedgwood cup designed by Ravilious has sold at auction for over £1,000.

The English Heritage (Cadw in Wales, and Historic Scotland) listing process is the main vehicle by which significant buildings are assessed and protected. As time rolls on, the finest are identified and hindsight shows us what has endured. The 30 year rule prevents any younger building from being listed (except in exceptional circumstances). The current reappraisal and appreciation of mid-1970s architecture is stimulating interest in that period.

Demolition practice and environmental and health and safety laws have changed how material is salvaged. The ease of salvage diminished when hand-dismantling gave way to dynamite and huge hydraulic crushers. Nevertheless, increasing value makes careful dismantling financially viable. Unfortunately, architectural theft has been an unwelcome side effect, so all your purchases should be made from a recognised dealer.

To make money, you need to read and predict how demographic, social or geographic influences

The interior of Swiss Cottage library by Sir Basil Spence showing the original furniture in situ

Removed during renovation work, the Spence desks are worth £500 each. Their provenance adds interest and value

may influence the market. For example, the shift to self-employment and changing working patterns has brought about a merging of home and office. Office furniture, like the Eames aluminium group designs, now sits happily in the living room, and warehouses have been converted into open-plan apartments making a virtue of bare brick and exposed joists. I recently bought an Eames aluminium group chair from a second-hand shop for £40. New ones are still being manufactured and sell for over £1,000.

New materials stimulate new designs, each bringing exciting opportunities but also conservation nightmares. Increasingly, items are designed with built-in obsolescence. To ensure that your antique of the future is going to last, familiarise yourself with the limitations and degradation of the material. I have lost money on plywood that delaminated, plastics that scratched, cracked and decomposed, and glue bonds that broke.

The key to any architectural piece's commercial value – as with any collectable – is condition, rarity, originality and innovation. Prototypes and early examples illustrating a design evolution will always be the most interesting, rarest and hence most valuable. Many pieces were designed by architects for specific projects and only later put into wider production. Manufacturers change, too, with companies buying production licences, or maybe a design will be subtly altered to avoid copyright infringement. Know what you are buying and who made it, and steer clear of worthless copies.

The provenance of a design is important. I recently bought furniture designed exclusively for Swiss Cottage Library by the architect Sir Basil Spence. Photos published at the time in *Architectural Review* showed the layout and gave information about design concept, costs and materials. The confirmed provenance will help when I sell the furniture – and will help any future seller.

KITCHENS

English Rose Kitchens, manufactured by CSA Industries, are a prime example of a well-designed product, superbly constructed and enduringly usable. Made from aluminium, these kitchens were the apogee of 1950s interior design. CSA Industries were one of the first companies to integrate appliances into kitchen design and so the products stand up well today. I would much rather have an English Rose kitchen than a MDF carcass designed to be disposable. When manufactured, English Rose kitchens were very expensive – the equivalent to Bulthaup or Smallbone today. But it is possible to pick up a second-hand English Rose from a salvage yard for around £500, although it may require restoration.

We relocated the kitchen illustrated from Rolls Royce's corporate headquarters, where it had 40 years' service, to a client's west London flat. A few cabinet doors were resprayed but otherwise the units were perfect. I challenge anyone to get as much life out of an IKEA kitchen. Our client paid a total of about £3,000 for the entire kitchen units, cupboards and worktop, comparable to a cheap, off-the-peg set at a DIY store. But the English Rose units will last longer and could even be relocated again. In time, they will also gain status and value as design classics.

The 1950s English Rose kitchen is full of period charm, and is worth about £3,000

A recreation of an 1890s bathroom

A coloured suite from the 1930s – sure to make a comeback! Price about £800–£1,200

BATHROOMS

The great Victorian sanitary engineers, Thomas Crapper and George Jennings, put their names on some spectacular plumbing fittings. Water closets with ornate transfer patterns, or with dolphin heads moulded into the design, are now very valuable. In the dark days of post-war building, many Victorian and Edwardian sanitary fittings were smashed as they were considered valueless. Now seen as one of the great pioneers of domestic sanitation, Thomas Crapper's name has become synonymous with his products, which are, consequently, highly collectable.

The pastel shade suites of the Deco years produced by companies such as Standard, were available with colour names like 'Claire de Lune Blue', 'Ming Green' and 'Rose du Barry'. They are still being thrown out. Ensure suites are complete and in good order as it is difficult to replace colour-matched items. Ten years ago, they were not appreciated, but now the market is established. A whole suite – wc, cistern, pedestal basin, maybe bidet, and bath – can be had for £400 to £800, but this is set to rise. The more traditional Victorian claw-and-ball foot bath costs £500 to £2,000.

The avocado, chocolate and butterscotch suites of the 1970s normally had plastic or fibreglass baths of inferior quality to the enamelled cast iron of earlier times and therefore have lasted less well. But who is to say that fashion may not yet favour them?

Another item of sanitaryware set to become a classic is the Vola tap designed by architect Arne Jacobson. Already recognised as a design icon, it ticks all the right boxes for a future antique; designed by a famous name, built to the highest standard, expensive to buy new, so not too common, and above all practical. Expect to pay about £450 for a new one.

WINDOWS

The slim metal section of Crittal windows is synonymous with Modernist architecture. The proportions of horizontal panes from the mid-century are so much finer than the chunky lifeless U-PVC that is taking over our towns and cities. I long for the day when the elegant metal frames are back in vogue. Problems with reuse include lack of insulation from single glazing, matching the sizes and rust.

Domestic stained glass, normally from the top sash of 1920s and 30s suburban houses, has a ready market but can be expensive to repair if damaged. The most commonly available windows are sash panes from 1930s suburban homes with floral or sunrise designs; these cost from about £30 to £100 a pane.

DOORS

The post-war fashion for clean lines and surfaces saw many a panelled door hardboarded over or removed. As the Victorians were inclined to decorate every surface, domestic doors were never intended to be left unpainted. I am glad that paint has had a revival. Original doors, like most other fittings, always benefit a period property.

FIREPLACES

The most established area of architectural antiques is the fireplace. Fireplaces were the most ornate and expensively decorated items in the house, made from the finest materials like marble, carved timber and stone. Grand Georgian chimney pieces in white statuary and sienna marble can be worth more than the average house, but it is also possible to find beautiful pieces for the more modest budget. A Victorian cast iron fireplace will cost about £800.

Resources

Further reading

www.salvo.co.uk is the most comprehensive website. Salvo is a trade network detailing all aspects of architectural salvage. They also publish a trade newspaper and price guide book.

Salvage Style: Home & Garden Projects Using Reclaimed Architectural Details, Joe Rhatigan and Dana Irwin, Lark Books, 2001

Museums

The Brooking Collection, Guildford, Surrey T: 01483 504555 or **The Brooking Collection**, University of Greenwich Dartford, Kent T: 020 8331 9897 www.dartfordarchive.org.uk/technology/art_brooking.shtml
Victoria and Albert Museum, London SW7 T: 020 7942 2000 www.vam.ac.uk
The Geffrye Museum, London E2 T: 020 7739 9893 www.geffrye-museum.org.uk
The Burrell Collection, Glasgow T: 0141 287 2550 www.clyde-valley.com/glasgow/burrell.htm

Sotheby's Sussex (01403 833500) have a twice yearly architectural sale of garden antiques and architectural items like fireplaces
Thos. Wm Gaze & Son have five dedicated architectural sales a year
Diss Auction Rooms, Diss, Norfolk T: 01379 650306 www.twgaze.com

TIMELINE

The value of a single item, such as Thomas Crapper's high level cistern, may be used as a barometer. In 1900, his Chelsea shop would have sold you a 'No 814 Valveless Water Waste Preventer' for one pound and sixpence (£1.02). In 1935, this same, rather dated cistern cost two pounds and seven shillings (£2.35). Still in production in 1955, although hopelessly anachronistic and old fashioned, it then cost four pounds, one shilling and sixpence (£4.07). In 1985, one sold for £1,500. Back in production in 1999, a new one cost £445. Today, its value restored would be about £650.

One of Thomas Crapper's innovative sanitary devices, now back in production

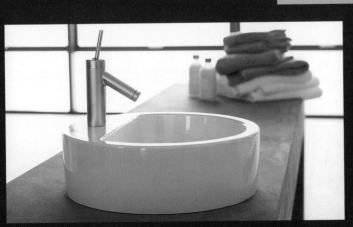

Starck Puro single lever basin mixer (10011), about £300

CRYSTAL BALL

Study today's design publications for tomorrow's antiques. Philippe Starck is a world renowned architect and designer, with a strong and highly recognisable personal style which almost guarantees that his work will appreciate in the future. Look out for his chrome Axor taps, costing about £300 for the basin mixer and £530 for the bath and shower mixer.

13

RUPERT VAN DER WERFF ON

GARDEN STATUARY, ORNAMENTS AND TOOLS

TIM WONNACOTT

Rupert van der Werff was appointed head of Sotheby's Garden Statuary department while I was chairman. I was delighted with his appointment and subsequent success. The department is the only specialist facility in the auction world, and is set in beautiful walled gardens in West Sussex. It is the market leader in this growing area for collectors and garden enthusiasts.

The term garden antiques will probably conjure up the image of a statue seen in some Arcadian setting. Eighteenth-century pieces tend to cost tens of thousands of pounds, but the majority of pieces at dealers or in auctions date from the late nineteenth and twentieth centuries. Most were made in quantity, helping keep prices more modest.

THE GARDEN MARKET

The market for garden antiques has only been recognised for the last twenty years, but has already expanded and matured. Some pieces have become classics, such as the Compton pots, Bromsgrove Guild figures and Haws watering cans. Many other items are beginning to be looked upon more seriously, like Lefcoware and Doulton.

Alongside garden decoration is a world of basic everyday items now called gardenalia. In the past of little interest to the collector, this category includes garden-related, manufactured items ranging from the ordinary robust garden tool to the more delicate seed packet.

When it comes to identifying investment potential in garden statuary, there are five fundamentals to consider – quality, design, condition, material and rarity. These separate the good from the bad, and the higher a piece scores in each category, the more likely it is to do well in the future.

Defining the necessary criteria for collecting normally includes an understanding of how much is available – too much and interest is likely to be ordinary; too little and the product may be too scarce for collectors to bother. Can one research the manufacturers? Can the range be referenced through original catalogues? Is the market affordable for new collectors? Is there a sense of development of style against a backdrop of social change? And, perhaps most important, is the area fashionable, or likely to be in the future? The answer to all these questions is yes. Garden museums are a good starting point. Manufacturers, such as Haws, are still in business and may help with research into their earlier products.

This still new area allows the creation of an interesting collection for little outlay but with the potential of a growing return on your investment. It is still possible to buy early twentieth-century tools for £5, and scarcer implements for under £50. In recent years, prices have risen as gardening has captured public interest. Collectors may find themselves in competition with gardeners, who admire the early twentieth-century products manufactured in England and appreciated all over the world. There is already a developing export market for useable old tools.

Stay clear of broken, badly rusted or poor tools. Look for quality products, notably from Sheffield, but also from Birmingham. Understand the quality of steel used in the manufacture. Some items were made to last more than one lifetime.

Look for products stamped with the manufacturer's name and trademark.

C. T. Skelton of Sheffield presented 35 different types of spades and forks in their 1927 catalogue. These included a number known by the county or regional area where they originated and acquired their popular form. The majority will cost between £20 and £40; none will be in excess of £100. Other leading makers include Brades, Vaughn and Elwell. Smaller tools, such as trowels, hand forks and daisy grubbers, come in various styles, and appeal to those with less space.

Many hand tools are individual and can be a real pleasure to use. A good quality stainless steel trowel, advertised as being 'always sharp and clean even after being exposed to the weather', cost two shillings and ten pence (14p) in 1935. A sound example today, costing £5 to £15, will still give excellent service, and a selection of different forms will make a fascinating display. Expect to pay more for tools like daisy grubbers and dibbers. Grubbers from a dealer will cost between £20 and £40, dibbers rather less, at between £15 and £25.

A selection of mid-twentieth-century hand tools, including specialist trowels, hand forks, children's tin plate versions, a dibber and a daisy grubber. Between £5 and £30

Regarded as a vital implement of the gardener's armoury in the early twentieth century, five syringes by important makers, including Abol, Dron Wal, Mysto and Four Oaks. Circa 1920–50. Between £10 and £40

Although basic hedge trimmers are common, the collector will encounter unusual designs produced to make this chore easier. A good example is the 'Astor', made by the Flexa Lawnmower Company in the 1930s, and currently available for about £25 to £50. Another scarcer model was made by Spong. But perhaps the 'daddy' of these was the 'Little Wonder' mechanical hedge trimmer, a remarkable and dangerous looking device, with a series of cutting blades arranged over 40 inches and powered by a hand-turning wheel. A two-man version of some 60 inches in length was also available. It was expensive, costing almost £7 in 1938 when a gardener might earn half that amount for a week's work. The 'Little Wonder' was never popular due to its awkwardness, and, at farm and estate sales in the 1950s, an auctioneer might have struggled to get five shillings (25p). Today, you may be asked £200 or more for a good example, and the presence of its original packing box with accessories would probably double that figure.

Innovation in tools reflects social and economic changes in the early and mid twentieth century. Some products are practically unchanged from 100 years ago; others are similar but are made now from materials unimagined 50 years ago. Others once regarded as critical elements of every gardener's tool shed are now rarely used outside a specialist nursery.

A neglected area is insecticide sprayers and syringes. Large sections of 1920s and 1930s catalogues are devoted to these. Used for spraying a fine mist by florists, spraying insecticides, limewashing and disinfecting, perhaps the best makes were Four Oaks, whose 'Undentable' patent is a classic garden syringe, and the 'Abol' range of products, which were advertised to 'Last a Lifetime'

Pruning, chopping, lopping and trimming implements, including secateurs, pruning scissors, head of averruncutor (tree pruner), Astor hedge trimmers, shears and a Myticuttah pruner. Circa 1930–50. Between £10 and £50

and endorsed by the National Rose Society. Invariably well made, some in solid brass, they were expensive but you can still find examples for perhaps £5 or £10 rising to £30 or more for an 'Undentable'. There are other lesser known makers and the variety of nozzles and development of style contribute to investment potential.

Watering cans have become very popular. The twentieth century has produced some attractive examples, despite these being tin, galvanised iron or even aluminium. The typical British can is sometimes referred to as the Peter Rabbit type, although its form dates from the eighteenth century. Until a few years ago, you could buy a 1920s example complete with rose for under £5; today, you would probably be asked between £15 and £25.

The rose is important, as these were made in different sizes, depending on the manufacturer. Cans without roses are difficult to match with another maker's rose, so check any watering can has a rose you can detach and replace. The best English watering cans are almost certainly those

Stylish watering cans from the 1950s, including Spanish/French professional steel can, Haws greenhouse can, can for house use and a 'kettle' shape can. Between £15 and £50

made by Haws, whose range offers a collecting field in its own right. Haws' success was such that they had many imitators and the best way to identify a Haws product is by the trade mark medallion on the shoulder of the can. Haws moved several times, so it is possible to date the can approximately from the address on the medallion. Haws still manufacture cans in their distinct style and old examples are increasingly appreciated – a good can may be £20 and upward, and larger or early examples in good order could be £50 or more.

In recent years, an influx of watering cans, mainly from France, has opened our eyes to further pleasing styles. Many collectors are attracted to the distressed paintwork, so if you buy a can with old paint, keep it in that condition. Appealing old paintwork can add significant value and place the object in that indefinable category of a decorative object.

For those with unlimited space, there are big collectables, such as rollers, wheelbarrows and, of course, lawnmowers. Rollers are made in an enormous variety of designs, and some, namely those in cast iron, are extremely stylish. Prices are equally varied, from about £10 to £200.

How about collecting ephemera? Seed packets and packaging, nursery catalogues and photographs are vulnerable and easily lost, but precious as a backdrop to our wider knowledge. In a 2003 Sotheby's Sussex sale, approximately 800 early twentieth-century seed packets were sold and made between £2 and £4 each.

GARDEN ORNAMENTS

Garden decoration, whether statues, fountains, planters or seats, has to cope with the weather. This must be a prime consideration. Some materials, like metals, can be very successfully restored whilst others, like terracotta, are much harder to restore. Freezing temperatures are the most dangerous enemy to even the toughest stones. Make sure you protect your piece if there is a risk of frost.

Buying garden antiques is not as simple as the better the condition, the more desirable the piece will be. Perversely, often the charm of a piece will be increased by a weathered look. Most people prefer an old-seeming piece in their gardens rather than one that looks shiny and new. A composition stone finial has more appeal and value if it is slightly chipped and covered in moss. It is not unknown for a weathered piece to fetch more at auction than the cost of buying a new one. However, a chipped and stained terracotta figure will never be as desirable as a more pristine example.

Have a good look at your intended purchase and don't be afraid to ask if you are in doubt. It is better to pay more for a good piece: a reputable dealer or auctioneer will tell you if a piece has major faults or is in need of serious restoration. Some of the bewildering range of reproductions now available are excellent, like the work of Philip Thomasson, and will surely become collectable. Others, however, are purely of decorative value and interest.

It is hard to convey the quality of a piece in words. Pieces carved from stone can be judged by the standard of the carving and by the stone itself. Are there any natural flaws or colour variations, for example? The best stone was usually kept for

A pair of white marble early eighteenth-century satyrs.
Value £10,000–£15,000

the best pieces. Look for well-finished surfaces, whether in stoneware, cast iron or lead. Seam marks should be hand-finished and smooth. Rough edges or numerous large casting bubbles would not have been let out of the factory or marked down as seconds. Compton were one of the few companies who did strike their stamp if the item was of second quality. Quite how

A cast iron suite of furniture designed by Edward Bawden in the 1950s. Value £3,000–£5,000 at auction

appreciated their designs are becoming can be seen by the number of copies, in all sorts of materials. At the beginning of the twentieth century, the largest scroll pot cost one pound fifteen shillings; by the end, it was worth over £1,000.

Do not be put off by old and flaking paint finishes, particularly on cast iron pieces. The paintwork is not integral to the piece, but a decorative finish that can be changed. It is hard, however, to re-create the wonderful and desirable look of multi-layered, old flaky paint. It can also help distinguish an old piece from a modern copy. The wooden slats of seats can be replaced if needs

be; they are functional, so the value is not affected. Some cast iron seats, like those designed by Edward Bawden, and made during the middle of the twentieth century, can still be found in original condition. The strong design of the seat commands higher prices. Today, one should make £1,500 at auction; ten years ago this figure was nearer £300.

Many of the twentieth century's great designers and architects have designed pieces for the garden; if a design can be attributed to Archibald Knox, Edwin Lutyens or Christopher Dresser, the greater its appeal. There are still discoveries waiting to be made.

Resources

Further reading

Miller's Garden Antiques: How to Source and Identify, R van der Werff and J Rees, Octopus, 2003

Garden Ornament: 500 Years of History and Practice, George Plumtree, Thames and Hudson, 1989

Antiques from the Garden, Alistair Morris, Garden Art Press, 1999

Antique Garden Ornament, John Davis, Antique Collectors Club, 1991

English Leadwork, Lawrence Weaver, Benjamin Blom Inc, 1972

Further information

Architectural Heritage, Taddington, Glos
T: 01386 584414 www.architectural-heritage.co.uk

Flaxton Antique Gardens, Flaxton, York
T: 01904 468468 www.salvoweb.com/dealers/flaxton

Holloways, Suckley, Worcester
www.holloways.co.uk

Jardinique, Alton, Surrey
T: 01420 560055 www.jardinique.co.uk

Sotheby's Sussex, Billingshurst
T: 01403 833500 www.sothebys.com

Museums

The Ironbridge Gorge Museum, Telford, Shropshire
T: 01952 884391 www.ironbridge.org.uk

Museum of Garden History, London SE1
T: 020 7401 8865 www.cix.co.uk/~museumgh

National Museum of Gardening, Trevarno Estate, Cornwall
T: 01326 574274 www.trevarnoestateandgardens.co.uk

TIMELINE

Compton Pottery (or The Potters' Arts Guild) was founded in Surrey by Mary Watts in 1896. An eighteen-inch terracotta pot with scroll handles by Compton Pottery would have cost one pound five shillings when it was made in the 1920s. By the early garden statuary auctions in the 1980s, its price would have risen to £400 to £600. Now one in good order with a nice company stamp would cost between £1,000 and £1,500.

A pair of Liberty's terracotta planters, early twentieth century, manufactured by Compton. Value £2,000–£3,000

A pair of Lefcoware urns, worth £400–£600

CRYSTAL BALL

A good example would be a buff coloured, glazed earthenware urn, designed by Archibald Knox and manufactured by Lefcoware. The globular bowl has an everted rim, and a stylised, continuous frieze. The tapering, cylindrical stem goes down into a square base. Examples (stamped at the base of the bowl and on the top of the pedestal) can still be found for £300 to £400, which seems modest to me.

14

CLIVE FARAHAR ON
BOOKS & PUBLICATIONS:
FIRST EDITIONS, CARTOONS AND COMICS

TIM WONNACOTT

"Clive is the least bookwormish of men, despite a life spent entirely in the book trade. I love his gurgling laugh – and wicked way with words which almost completely disguises the depth of his knowledge. I recently flew back from Ulster with him after filming the *Antiques Roadshow* at Mount Stewart. I wonder what the passenger in Seat 13c thought of us nattering on about Winnie the Pooh while swilling back the G & T!"

The last hundred years have seen a remarkable change in the antiquarian and second-hand book trade, with the replacement in virtually every high street of old bookshops by charity shops. Oxfam, allegedly Europe's biggest retailer of second-hand books, says that the trade has doubled in the past four years. In 2002 they sold 12 million books and expect to have sold 15 million in 2003 in their 60 dedicated bookshops.

So the post-modern second-hand and antiquarian bookseller, who cannot compete, now has offices in less prominent positions, or works from home, using fax and internet. The pace of business is so fast that our ancestors wouldn't recognize it. The computer revolution has made it easier for the collector to compare prices, search for books and buy globally. It is wrong to believe that the end of the book is nigh; on the contrary, it is thriving.

The symptoms of bibliomania are everywhere. Thirty years ago, Richard Booth transformed Hay-on-Wye, a sleepy Welsh border town, into a mecca for book collectors. Starting with the old cinema, he bought or rented inexpensive shop premises left empty by recession and the coal industry's decline, and created a town dominated by books. What he pioneered has been copied in over 30 ventures worldwide, including in France, Norway, Malaysia and Scotland.

MODERN FIRST EDITIONS

The most notable rise in the last 25 years has been in modern first editions. The number of dedicated dealers has grown, particularly in the United States.

This market is, however, vulnerable to fashion. Before the 1930s Stock Market crash, John Galsworthy's *The Forsyte Saga* was selling for hundreds of pounds; today, however, a first edition may cost little more than £10. The late 1990s publishing phenomenon, J. K. Rowling's *Harry Potter* books, has taken the second-hand market by storm. Few copies have survived of the first, inexpensively produced *Harry Potter and the Philosopher's Stone*. But this small edition lit fires among readers and collectors alike. Prices are regularly quoted between £18,000 and £20,000, but, with subsequent editions and titles, the publishers made sure of good supply, reflected in lower prices.

Sir Arthur Conan Doyle's *The Hound of the Baskervilles*, normally selling at around £2,000, was sold in 1998 at auction for £72,000 because it had a dust wrapper. Once discarded after purchase, dust wrappers became the most important and artistic feature of the first edition market in the twentieth century, and vastly increase a book's value. A first edition, three-volume set of J. R. R. Tolkien's *The Lord of the Rings*, with dust wrappers, sells for around £20,000; without, it would make a fraction of that. Films play their part, too. Although there are plenty of copies of these modern books around,

The exterior of a booksellers in Hay-on-Wye, transformed by Richard Booth 30 years ago into a mecca for booklovers

they are rarely found in fine condition, for which the collector will pay a premium.

The 1960s drug culture had American writers Jack Kerouac and William Burroughs heading the Beat generation, which included poets and painters as well. The price of Kerouac's *On the Road* and Burroughs' *Naked Lunch* has risen over the years, as ageing hippies have become increasingly nostalgic and wealthy.

Signed presentation copies, copies with annotations or corrections by the author, or with small drawings by artists such as Arthur Rackham, all add value. In the late nineteenth century, the French pioneered the *Livre d'Artiste* movement, in which texts were secondary to the illustrations, with the artist involved with every aspect of the book. Picasso, Rouault, Miro and Chagall were notable exponents, and examples can be found from Germany, Spain, the USA and Great Britain. The finished product was a work of art, and the collector's interest is more in the artist than the text.

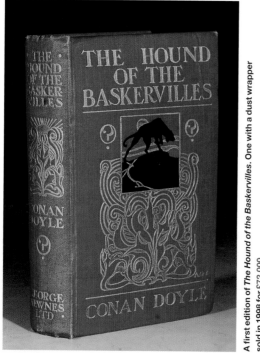

A first edition of *The Hound of the Baskervilles*. One with a dust wrapper sold in 1998 for £72,000

Superman comic, issue 1 from 1938. A copy of that first issue has made over US$60,000 at auction

Le Chef d'Oeuvre Inconnu by Balzac, illustrated by Picasso, Paris 1931. This *Livre d'Artiste* edition was sold at Sotheby's in 2002 for £22,500

COMICS AND COMIC ANNUALS

Comics and comic annuals have been a late twentieth-century growth area. By the 1960s, comic shops were springing up over America, arriving in Britain in the late 1970s and early 1980s. In America, Superman first appeared in *Action Comics* in 1938. Within the last five years, a copy of that first issue made over US$60,000 at auction. Batman debuted in the May 1939 edition of *Detective Comics*.

In Britain, our favourites, *Beano*, *Dandy*, *Topper* and, particularly, Rupert, appear head and shoulders above all others in popularity and price. As always, condition is crucial – prices not clipped, magic paintings not coloured in, and, of course, spines intact. Rupert was the *Daily Express*'s foil to the *Daily Mirror*'s cartoon Pip, Squeak and Wilfred, and the *Daily Mail*'s Teddy Tail. Mary Tourtel, wife of the *Express*'s night editor, wrote and drew Rupert from 1920 to 1935, handing over to Alfred Bestall, who carried on until 1972. The first Rupert annual, which came out in 1936, will make around £500 without a dust wrapper, and has made over £2,000 with one. Prices for Rupert are climbing. The Tartarus *Guide to First Edition Prices 1998–9* suggests prices for pre-war Rupert annuals of £200 to £300, but they are now making much more. Post-war annuals, from 1950–1960, quoted in guides at £50 to £100, are now making double at auction as the demand for fine copies grows. Any Bestall period volume is in great demand.

Beano, *Dandy* and *Topper*, from the D. C. Thomson stable, were all printed on inferior paper, which makes fine copies hard to find, but demand is strong. It seems that D. C. Thomson don't sell their original art work, but some from the Reverend Marcus Morris's *Eagle* has been sold through Christie's. A new saleroom in London, Comic Book Postal Auctions, holds sales of comics and annuals from across the world.

CHILDREN'S BOOKS

A book can be given to a child, read, played with, coloured, drawn in, enjoyed and loved. Or it can be put away on a shelf and remain pristine. The former is worth little commercially, the latter a lot. The collector will want the pristine because it is rarer; the child, in enjoying the book, has reduced its value. A. A. Milne's *Winnie the Pooh*, one of the most enduring titles of childhood, is now making over £1,000 for a fine first edition with dust wrapper. Thirty years ago, this not uncommon book would have made well under £100. Booksellers are now marking later

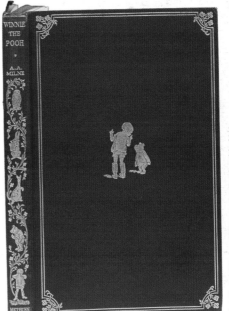

Fine first editions of *Winnie the Pooh*, with dust wrapper, are now making in excess of £1,000

The Big Noddy Book of 1959 can now make £95 at auction

AUTOGRAPH LETTERS AND MANUSCRIPTS

This has been an interesting market in the twentieth century. In the nineteenth century, autographs were massively collected. However, the signature from a letter was often all that was collected, but today's collectors are more interested in content than their forebears and one wonders what fascinating material was discarded.

One nineteenth-century collector stands out: that is Sir Thomas Phillipps, who amassed one of the most incredible collections of manuscripts and letters ever known. Now mostly dispersed, it fuelled countless auction sales in the second half of the twentieth century.

The market in the first half of the twentieth century was astonishingly weak. In the magnificent catalogues of Maggs Bros, published before the Second World War, one reads page after page of fabulous items, eruditely catalogued, priced at one and two guineas. The thrill of owning something written by a great author, soldier, poet, painter or explorer is understood by many.

After the Second World War, the market looked up, changing again by the late twentieth century as western material became harder to find. The collapse of the Soviet Union released much that had formerly been scarce. Interest in Russian royalty is immense, particularly in Tsar Nicholas II and his family, murdered in 1918.

The indiscretions, abdication and adulteries of British royalty have maintained public interest. Prices for photographs signed by Princess Diana soared after her death. In the following years, the trade realised that much on the market was coming from stocks held by the royal household, so prices have now gone down. However, there is

editions, depending on condition, over £100, when 30 years ago they would have been priced under £20.

Enid Blyton, so long outlawed from libraries for political incorrectness, is back and rising. Her early 1950s *Noddy Books* are making up to £100. *The Big Noddy Book* of 1959 makes £95. Her *Famous Five* books are also following in Noddy's footsteps.

Also worth considering are mechanicals – interactive books with slides to be pulled, pop-ups popped-up, and jigsaws made. In the 1920s the Bookano series of pop-up books were published. These were on cheap paper but are nonetheless very collectable. Prices vary between £50 to £100, depending on the title.

little doubting the worldwide enthusiasm for autographs. Unlike the Victorians, collectors want more than the signature; they want to feel the pulse of history between their hands. The postcard from the *Titanic*, the report from the Battle of Balaclava, the miseries and joys of pioneering, the inscrutable diplomatic manoeuvres in some corner of the globe, and the news from explorers – all are highly sought after. At a recent exhibition, we gave a showy display of signed photographs from royalty, politicians, the great and the good from around the world. A passing visitor remarked, 'My, you are well connected'. That is precisely what the collector wants – to be in closer communion with the past, holding a letter written and signed by Dickens or Browning, or an inscribed photograph of Princess Diana.

Newsreader Richard Baker tells an apocryphal story. Leaving Broadcasting House one day, he was approached by a little boy with autograph book and pen. As he was signing, he asked, 'Do you know who I am?' 'No,' replied the lad. 'But you will do for swaps.' So many of the autograph books that come into the *Antiques Roadshow* are just that – swaps of little commercial value.

In autographs, there are many pitfalls, from the secretary who signs for the boss, through to the autopen (a mechanical device that can repeatedly reproduce a signature with a pen), used by American presidents and British royalty from the early 1960s. Curiously, the late Queen Mother signed her own Christmas cards well into her nineties. Finally, when she became too infirm, she abandoned the pen in favour of a stamp. The only other time she had her cards stamped was in 1935, as Duchess of York, when she had 'flu.

Facsimile letters, again, can deceive. Especially

A signed photograph of Diana, Princess of Wales, from the collection of Clive Farahar and Sophie Dupré, £1,750

A postcard sent to Bert Pickett by Anne Perreault from the *Titanic*, 11 April 1912. Any *Titanic* postcard in good condition, dated 11 April, is likely to fetch up to £10,000 at auction

notorious are Churchill's 'Thanks for your good wishes on my birthday' notes that look as though they were handwritten on Downing Street notepaper. A London firm of auctioneers used to keep one pinned up at the reception desk in their book department, to demonstrate to hopeful clients how exactly their copy matched the one on the wall.

Resources

Further reading

Antiquarian Books: A Companion for Booksellers, Librarians and Collectors,
    P. Bernard (editor), Scholar Press, 1994
Comic Values Annual, The Comic Books Price Guide, Alex Malloy,
    Wallace-Homestead Book Company, Radnor, Pennsylvania, USA
A Bear's Life, Rupert, George Perry, Express Newspapers, 1985
Guide to First Edition Prices (Annual), R. B. Russell (editor),
    Tartarus Press

Specialist Book Auctioneers

Bloomsbury Book Auctions, London EC1
T: 020 7833 2636 www.bloomsbury-book-auct.com
Dominic Winter Book Auctions, Swindon, Wilts
T: 01793 611340 www.dominic-winter.co.uk
Malcolm Phillips, Comic Book Auctions, London NW1
T: 020 7424 0007 Comicbook@compuserve.com

On Disc

American Book Prices Current, Bancroft Parkman Inc
PO Box 1236, 62 Old Litchfield Road, Washington, CT 06973 USA
e-mail: abpc@snet.net
A 20 year listing to the present of book and manuscript prices at auction, across the world.

Internet sites

www.ilab-lila.com
www.abebooks.co.uk (used books)
www.abebooks.com (rare books and first editions)
www.alibris.com
www.a1books.com
www.amazon.com
www.ebay.co.uk
www.farahardupre.co.uk

Booksellers, Associations & Magazines

Maggs Bros Ltd, Modern First Editions, Livre d'Artiste, London W1
T: 020 7493 7160 www.maggs.com
Nigel Williams, Modern First Editions and Children's Books.
London WC2 T: 020 7836 7757 www.nigelwilliams.com
Simon Finch, Modern Books, London W11
T: 020 7792 3303 www.simonfinch.com
Antiquarian Booksellers Association, London W1
T: 020 7439 3118 www.aba.org.uk
Antiquarian Booksellers Association of America, New York, USA
T: (212) 944 8291 www.abaa.org
Book and Magazine Collector, Diamond Publishing Group Ltd
Ealing, London W5 T: 020 8579 082
Antiquarian Book Monthly, PO Box 97, High Wycombe
Buckinghamshire, HP14 4GH

TIMELINE

A pre-war Rupert would have retailed for about two shillings and sixpence. I have one from 1951 which cost four and ninepence. By 1960, nobody would have bothered to pay more than a few pence for an old Rupert. The market got going when Alfred Bestall's retirement in 1972 fostered nostalgia for his period among collectors. By 1980, prices for early Rupert Annuals were between £25 and £50, and, by 2004, £500 plus. In one spectacular auction result in the 1990s, a mint copy of the first Rupert annual, in an unheard of dust wrapper, made over £2,000.

CRYSTAL BALL

A good tip for investment has to be modern pop-up books. In the 1970s and 1980s, Jan Pienkowski published his famous pop-up books, including *Haunted House*, which even made noises. Towards the end of the century, there were many imitators, and rashes of pop-ups and movable books appeared, and were remaindered. In time, these excellent but fragile books will surely make their way on to collectors' shelves.

Jan Pienkowski's pop-up books from the 1970s and 1980s, like *Haunted House*, may well be good investments for the future

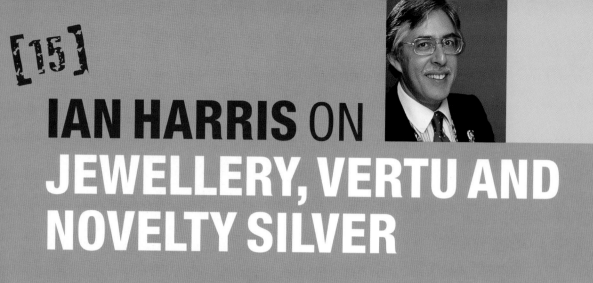

[15]

IAN HARRIS ON
JEWELLERY, VERTU AND
NOVELTY SILVER

TIM WONNACOTT

Ian has always struck me as an immensely stylish man, a man of taste and discernment. As proprietor of one of London's leading jewellers with over 50 years' experience in the business, he will have seen more jewellery and precious objects than any other person I know.

No period or style arrives without looking back to what went before. But, although there is virtually nothing new, the twentieth century does mark a turning point in design and manufacturing, use of materials, and sales and promotional methods.

Art Nouveau is the most characteristic early twentieth-century style, although it began the decade before and had early seventeenth-century Dutch origins. There are radical national differences: French and Belgian Art Nouveau featured whip-like scrolling tendrils, while the Scottish and Austrian Art Nouveau of Charles Rennie Mackintosh and Joseph Hoffman was more rectangular. English design was influenced by both, as well as by William Morris's Arts and Crafts movement.

JEWELLERY AND VERTU

Traditional design produced Edwardian or Belle Epoque jewellery and vertu (small, finely made decorative objects), which is extremely delicate and pretty. Sometimes called the Festoon style, it borrowed Robert Adam's swags and festoons, classical urns and flaming torches, Cupid's bow and arrows, and laurel borders from the late eighteenth century.

This delicacy was achieved by the move from silver to platinum for setting diamonds. Platinum had been known and used since the eighteenth century, but only to a limited degree; extremely hard, it melts at a higher temperature than gold, so is difficult to solder. These technical difficulties were overcome around 1900, a crucial date in jewellery. Mostly 'white' gems like diamonds and pearls then began to be set so that the metal became close to invisible. Until 1900, settings for diamond jewellery had been gold at the back, with a veneer of silver at the front. Initially, jewellers followed this method, substituting platinum for silver. When they realized that this was an unnecessary complication, they started to use platinum only. This is a good marker for earlier, rather than later, Edwardiana. Jewellery from the period is now very costly: the diamond and platinum spider pendant illustrated would cost between £3,000 and £5,000.

Fabergé is the supreme example of a designer who looked back to the late eighteenth century. He was extraordinarily dedicated to perfection of craftsmanship and technique, and insisted on his workshop achieving it. It helped, of course, to have a cheap labour force and an extremely wealthy clientele, to whom novelty and workmanship were more important than cost.

This cheap labour/wealthy clientele relationship is also important in understanding jewellery made before 1939 (the finest period, in my view, of jewellery design). Until the dawn of the welfare state, you had to be more than good at your job or you were sacked, and you starved. This tough regime produced craftsmen who started in

Belle Epoque festoon style pendant by Gautrait, Paris, in his typical style, £10,000

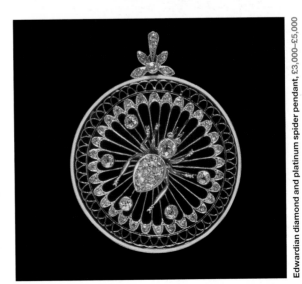

Edwardian diamond and platinum spider pendant, £3,000–£5,000

Art Nouveau brooch in the style of Lalique, £7,000–£10,000

Art Deco colourful Buddha-type pendant, showing oriental influence, £25,000

the workshop at fourteen, doing menial jobs, and, over the traditional seven-year apprenticeship, learned to turn out work of the highest quality.

Throughout the twentieth century, and from the start of the industrial revolution, jewellery, silver and novelties have also been produced for the mass market. The main centre of this trade in Britain was Birmingham, turning out hundreds of thousands of silver bar brooches, name brooches, gold back-and-front lockets, Mizpah (message) brooches for those to be separated by war or service overseas. Most are fully hallmarked, so can be dated exactly and the makers identified. Good collectables, many of them sell for less than £100 or even £50.

Something else often seen, but often not recognised, is Suffragette jewellery, in colours green (peridot/demantoid garnet), white (diamonds/pearls) and violet (amethyst), supposedly standing for Give Women Votes. Pendants made of pearl, amethyst and green enamel cost now from £200.

'Edwardian' covers the period between 1900 and 1914, co-existing with Art Nouveau and Arts and Crafts work, desirable today but less popular then. The acknowledged masters of Art Nouveau include Fouquet, Gaillard and René Lalique, the greatest artist–jeweller of his time. For these makers, the designs were more important than gems, but, unfortunately, the pieces tended to cost as much as fully gem-set jewellery. A genuine Lalique Art Nouveau brooch might now cost as much as £50,000. As most clients, for the same money, preferred flash to artistry, the sufficiently wealthy and appreciative were relatively few, accounting for the shortage of good Art Nouveau jewellery today.

There was, however, a large market for mass-produced, inexpensive Art Nouveau jewellery. Companies like Murrle, Bennett & Co imported from Germany small items in nine carat gold or silver set with blister pearls, amethysts, turquoise or other inexpensive stones, or enamel, which were sold by Liberty's and other outlets. Silver pieces can be bought for around £300, while the nine carat gold ones will cost from £500 to £1,000. Similar items were produced in Birmingham by the now very collectable designer and manufacturer Charles Horner. Prices for his work are similar.

Boundaries are often blurred between Art Nouveau and Arts and Crafts, but the latter had the more lasting influence, going on well into the 1930s with such makers as Sibyl Dunlop and Dorrie Nossiter. Their work was large and colourful with many bright but inexpensive gemstones and pearls, mostly set in silver, which now cost between £750 and £2,500, depending on size and decoration. *The Studio* magazine had regular design competitions for amateur jewellers, silversmiths and enamellers. As a handmade look was integral to the style, pieces were not expected to be technically perfect. Stylish, unsigned pieces, made by such skilful amateurs, can be bought for between £100 and £500.

1918 brought a reaction against war-time austerity. Even before the war, Cartier were producing pieces with a Deco feel, using coral, onyx and rock crystal. The Exposition des Arts Decoratifs in Paris in 1925 gave a name to a style that was already well established. It was colourful, geometric, fascinated by the exotic influences of the Orient, India, South America, and, of course, Egypt. The French undoubtedly led the fashion for Deco and produced some of the most sophisticated and high quality pieces, not only in jewellery, but in silver, furniture, painting, fabrics and other decorative arts.

Cartier was the biggest producer of fine Deco jewellery and objects, but all the well-known French jewellers produced similar items of similar quality; it's just that Cartier's greater output, exhibitions, books and publicity, especially the Windsor sale, have made them best known of their contemporaries. English makers of fine jewellery did not have their own shops but sold through retailers, so their pieces are seldom signed. Expect to pay double the price for anything with confirmed Cartier provenance.

SILVER

There's a dearth of early twentieth-century novelty silver. The inspiration of the 1870s and 1880s seems to have died. You get little pepper pots caricaturing politicians, and novelty vesta cases, but silverware designs generally hark back to the eighteenth century. A typical example is the Queen Anne teapot. Oval, and with the lower half fluted, it is actually a bastardized great-grandson of the 1790s and no relation to Queen Anne whatever. A piece of commercially made silver like this costs between £200 and £300.

Silver in the Art Nouveau and Arts and Crafts taste was produced by the Guild of Handicrafts. Typical examples are very collectable, such as round sweet dishes with whip-like extended handles, which now cost between £1,500 and £2,500. In Birmingham, A. E. Jones found a way of producing extra lightweight silver which was sold inexpensively. Designs that were more Medieval

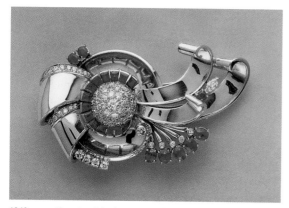

1940s smooth and polished gem-set gold brooch, £3,000–£5,000

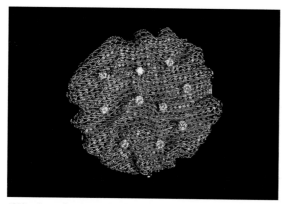

1950s wirework, gemset, £1,500–£2,500

Examples of work by Andrew Grima, the best from the 1960s and 1970s, £8,000–£10,000

Revival than Art Nouveau or Arts and Crafts were produced by the partnership of Omar Ramsden and Alwyn Carr. Many pieces were made to commission, and chased with presentation inscriptions. This silver has an irregular hammered finish, which could not be done by machine. Ramsden pieces are hand-raised; commercial pieces would have been die-stamped or spun and then quickly hammered over.

Ramsden and Carr split up in 1919. Both continued independently, but Ramsden continued up to 1939, so he is more collected. A Ramsden six-inch diameter wooden mazer bowl, with silver rim and foot, would have cost a few hundred in the 1950s. The price is now nearer £5,000.

Other interesting 1930s silversmiths include R. E. Stone. Deco designs were produced commercially in London, Birmingham and Sheffield. Broadly speaking, the makers in Birmingham and Sheffield were highly mechanised and commercial, turning out pieces in quantity. London, however, continued to be dominated by artist-craftsmen, producing one-offs or much smaller numbers.

Ramsden prices were pushed up to very high levels a few years ago, but are now somewhat more realistic. It is always best to go for the best-known names, even if something equally good is available by a less well-known maker at a lesser price.

AFTER THE SECOND WORLD WAR

The Second World War ended most jewellery and silver making in Europe, although the French houses managed a modest output. The 1940s, or retro, style, which really began in the mid-1930s, was therefore led by America. In stark contrast to the geometry of Deco, it featured polished pink gold in flamboyant scrolls set with large aquamarines or citrines, with rubies and diamonds. Coloured stones of no great quality were used for some very flamboyant, large and spectacular pieces. Even in America, there was difficulty sourcing newly mined stones from around the world, so they made do with what they had. Most American jewellery is fourteen karat – a useful way of identifying it, as they spell their carats with a K, as opposed to the general European standard for quality jewellery of eighteen carat. They also tended to use white gold as much as platinum. Makers like Oscar Heymann (an outstanding craftsman whose pieces now sell for $10,000 upwards), Verdura, Seaman Schepps and others produced high quality pieces of striking design. Their designers had often worked before the war for the major French houses. Liberated from gem costs, costume jewellery could be high fashion, and the best was well made. You may find an unsigned and unremarkable piece from this period at a Sunday fair for as little as £10; signed pieces by better known makers will cost between £200 and £500.

After the smooth gold-work of the 1940s came the twisted wire-work of the 1950s. Europe was reviving, and once more led design. The 1960s and 1970s saw a return to texture, and also the rise of Italian designers and manufacturers. They specialized in flexible gold-work chains and bracelets, and also enamelled brooches. Chains are sold by weight, at about £25 to £30 per gram. Enamelled brooches cost from £500 to £1,500 and are still undervalued in my view. An outstanding designer from this period was Andrew Grima, but 'designer jewellery' is a very specialised collecting area.

For collectors with modest budgets, I would suggest good Arts and Crafts jewellery, preferably named, or even fine costume jewellery. Silver has had ups and downs, but Omar Ramsden will survive. Quality always shows; but condition is equally important. If you feel uncertain, rely on a reputable dealer. You will pay a premium, but good advice is worth it. Get a list of vetted specialist dealers from LAPADA, or visit good quality fairs. And there is the odd treasure to be found at Sunday antiques fairs round the country.

Resources

Further reading

N. Bloom & Son produce an annual catalogue, available on request, or viewable at www.nbloom.com. It also contains information about anniversaries, the legendary virtues of gem-stones, comparative ring sizes and how to buy and sell. A longer-term project is to archive all our old catalogues on to our site. These go back 25–30 years, and have been faithfully collected by some of our customers. It is interesting to see that you could have bought a pretty Giuliano enamel heart brooch with small cabochon rubies round the edge from one of our earlier catalogues for £195!

Antique and Twentieth Century Jewellery: A Guide for Collectors, Vivienne Becker, N A G Press, 1990.

Concise and informative on periods, styles, materials, techniques, and better known makers of the nineteenth and twentieth centuries.

There are many other, more specialised books on antique jewellery and silver on www.amazon.co.uk

Further information

The Goldsmiths Company, London EC2 (020 7606 7010 or www.thegoldsmiths.co.uk, is one of the few livery companies that still has legal authority over its trade, and it does a great deal to encourage contemporary jewellers and silversmiths by promoting their work at very popular selling exhibitions at the Hall. Details on their website.

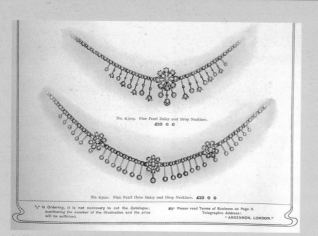

An illustration from a Goldsmiths and Silversmiths Co Catalogue of circa 1910 of an eighteen carat gold, diamond and pearl daisy and drop necklace, £10

TIMELINE

This eighteen carat gold, diamond and pearl daisy and drop necklace would have cost £10 in 1910. Prices didn't change much through the 1930s and 1940s, but, by 1950, the same necklace would probably have cost about £250. The price of jewellery has not risen in a continuous curve. After the late 1980s boom years, the trade hit a recession in the 1990s, and prices have risen little over the last decade or so. Nevertheless, that necklace today would probably sell for about £3,000.

The same necklace, retail price in 2003, approximately £3,000

CRYSTAL BALL

David Hensel is an interesting contemporary jeweller. His rings typically retail for around £1,250, very different from the £5,000 or so charged by other makers. Hensel's work often has a sinister quality, but I am fascinated by his silver and gold settings, with hard stones which, unusually, he carves himself. If, in the future, he receives the recognition he deserves, his work will repay collecting.

For the future: a selection of contemporary rings by David Hensel, all selling at £1,250 each

RUPERT MAAS ON
BRITISH PICTURES

TIM WONNACOTT

> Strangely, pictures seem to attract the tallest experts! Both Henry Wyndham, Chairman of Sotheby's, and Richard 'Ricky' Roundell, Deputy Chairman of Christie's, tower above the rest of us, alongside Rupert Maas, who is six foot six and a half inches! From their lofty perch, they must see art from a different perspective! An *Antiques Roadshow* veteran, Rupert is a second-generation West End dealer, who has earned a considerable reputation as a champion of twentieth-century painting.

'About things on which the public thinks long it commonly attains to think right.'
SAMUEL JOHNSON

The public hasn't thought long enough about twentieth-century British painting yet. So, if you want to collect it, you can make up the rules. Think of it as exploring a large garden with a variety of different plants, some beautiful, some interesting and some both. Many good plants are hidden under others; some that seem lovely at first turn out to be dull. Many people haven't the confidence to choose amongst the variety on display, and so follow like sheep.

You don't actually need to know anything about art. I now try hard to forget what I learned at university, the more to rely upon my instinct. Through the *Antiques Roadshow*, I meet many non-professionals with a naturally discerning eye. Conversely, I often meet academics who wouldn't know a good picture if it got up and bit them.

Taste is a matter of instinct. There's no magic; it's not dependent on training or even knowledge. The discipline is in recognizing the tiny voice that says yes and acting upon it. This demands confidence, even arrogance, for you may be backing your eye against received opinion.

What do we learn from these platitudes? A thousand don'ts and only one do – buy what you like. You cannot successfully invest in pictures unless you have some feeling for them. Even then, you might have to wait 25 years before you can realise your assets.

And you can't easily make money out of discoveries. It is too risky. My father always used to say there are two kinds of picture dealer: Constable hunters and dealers. You can either work yourself into the ground, driving 80,000 miles a year looking for that under-catalogued Constable to make your fortune, or you can trade at smaller margins, building up a good business. Dealers are only useful insofar as they are selling pictures more likely than others to increase in value over time. The collector should be the winner simply because he holds the stock for longer – and his reward will be not just the increase in value but also the pleasure of ownership.

POINTERS FOR COLLECTORS

- Always remember that it is better to have one good picture than ten mediocre ones.
- You should never buy an artist because he is popular, or in anticipation of his death or an exhibition.
- There is no such thing as a bargain in the art market (which doesn't mean your picture will not prove a good investment).
- It is worth paying a premium to get what you want and it's best to ignore saleroom estimates. Be prepared to make mistakes and sell when you tire of a picture.
- Ask close friends their opinion but be confident in your own eye.
- Important, too, to remember that the opportunity of a lifetime must be grasped in the lifetime of the opportunity.
- Make a friend of an art dealer, as he will save you money in the long run.

ABSTRACT PAINTING

The biggest problem most people have with the twentieth century is abstract painting, which began to appear in British art after Roger Fry's revolutionary exhibition, 'Manet and the Post-Impressionists', in London in 1917. No one has a special gift for understanding abstraction – if certain colours and shapes together could be said to be pleasing or stimulating, then the picture works. I was taught a trick by a great art historian: when confronted by an abstract, screw up your eyes until it is only a blur. You will be surprised how much more accessible it becomes!

I am reminded of the story of a young artist who, spotting Turner at the Royal Academy after a lecture on the theory of painting, asked the great man what he thought of it all. After a long pause, Turner said, 'It's a rum go, painting,' and went on his way. If he didn't know, what chance have the rest of us got? So, have a go, find a picture that does something for you, and buy it.

WHAT TO BUY

Drawings and watercolours are a good way into the masters of the period, if you must have a work by a sought-after artist, and haven't the budget for an oil (it's not worth buying a bad oil). Drawings from any early twentieth-century student of the Slade School are covetable – hard to find, but not too expensive. Everyone has heard of Augustus John. However, until recently, fewer had heard of his fellow student, Henry Lamb, a versatile and subtle artist whose prices lag way behind those of John. A particularly beautiful example is an oil on tempera, *Two Nudes of 1911*, which echoes Picasso's blue period. This picture cannot have cost more

Two Nudes, 1911, by Henry Lamb RA, LG, 1883–1960. Oil and tempera on canvas. 26½ x 21 in. Now worth at least £250,000

Flowers and Gloves, 1909, by Sir William Nicholson, 1872–1949. Oil on canvas. Signed and dated lower right; signed on stretcher verso. 25⁵⁄₈ x 21³⁄₈ in. Now valued in excess of £250,000

than £1,000 when first sold. It is worth at least £300,000 now. But a drawing by Lamb can be bought for £2,000 to £3,000, although a really good one might cost £6,000.

If drawings are a reasonable route to owning work by a sought-after artist, then watercolours are still much less expensive than oils – and in colour! The trouble with watercolours has been that they didn't last – if they escaped damp, mould and acid attack from bad framing materials, they were faded to invisibility by light. An important recent innovation may revolutionise the market – ultra-violet light rejecting glass. Ordinary glass rejected about 25 per cent of the UV that fades watercolours, but the new glass rejects over 95 per cent. We can start to hang watercolours in our homes again without fear of watching our investment disappear. Illustrated is a beauty by Paul Nash. It can't have been worth

Empty Beach, Rye, 1922, by Paul Nash, 1889–1946. Watercolour and pencil on paper. Signed and dated lower right. 14 x 21 in. Now worth £30,000

Venetian Nights, James McBey, 1883–1959. Etching. Still inexpensive at £5,000

A Corner of My Garden, 1936, by Sir Stanley Spencer, 1891–1959. Oil on canvas. Signed and dated. 30 x 20 in. Sold for £120,000 in 2003

more than £2,000 in the early 1980s, and is now worth £30,000.

Despite the onset of Modernism after 1917, it took a time for the painterly values learned by the immediately post-Victorian generation of artists to be forgotten. Father and son William and Ben Nicholson are illustrative of this change. Both artists' work is now far too expensive for the casual investor, but it was not always so. In the early 1980s, this William Nicholson was worth about £25,000. Now it is worth ten times as much. In 1990 an oil by William's son, Ben, was probably worth a maximum of £50,000, but it is now valued at three times that. This may seem like a fantastic rise, but in the early 1980s it was worth close on £1 million. The Japanese went mad for this kind of Nicholson at that time, and when their financial markets collapsed, so did his prices.

Stanley Spencer is now regarded as one of the greats. A million pounds is needed for one of his quirkily painted religious subjects or the savagely intimate portrayals of himself and his wife. However, Spencer had other, less introspective subjects, such as the series of extraordinary

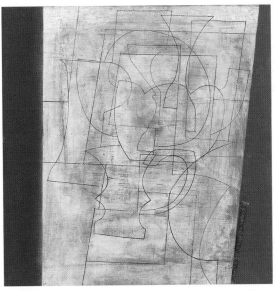

Green Chisel, 1955, Ben Nicholson OM, 1894–1982. Oil and pencil on canvas. Signed, titled and dated verso. 24 x 24 in. Now worth £175,000

paintings of gardens from the 1930s, which are just as desirable – perhaps even more so because they are easier to live with. The one illustrated could have been yours for £120,000 in 2003.

So much for the mainstream and the expensive – what about off the beaten track? The etching revival between the wars threw up some great works. You should not have to spend above £1,000 for most and £5,000 for the very best. An etching by James McBey, such as *Venetian Nights*, might have been worth £400 at the time it was made, but you could have bought it for £30 in the 1960s. Even now it is cheap to buy at about £5,000.

SPOTTING TRENDS

Some areas of painting remain inaccessible – the black and tan sludgescapes of the 1950s, for example, or simpering South Seas maidens in puce and pink. The most famous painter of these was Vladimir Tretchikoff. It was once said that the only artist to have made more money than Tretchikoff was Picasso, and certainly, after 1952, when he decided to sell mass-produced prints of his paintings, Tretchikoff's phenomenal success destroyed his reputation as a serious artist.

The LSD-induced polychromatic fantasies of the 1960s can be amusing, while the 1970s gave rise to what I call the 'Ford Capri' school of painting – androgynous aliens airbrushed into catsuits. If you enjoy any of these areas, then doubtless there is a hierarchy of excellence amongst them and, using your eye, you can still pick the best from them relatively inexpensively. I came across a C. R. Howe, who is terrifically awful in a marvellous way. One day, my sarcasm will be viewed as blinkered conditioning, and your prescience will doubtless be rewarded.

Fantasy Landscape, C. R. Howe, 1972. Oil on canvas laid on board. Signed and dated. Sold for £400 in 2001

Twin Peaks, Tobit Roche, 2001. Oil on canvas. Signed and dated verso. 35 x 62 in. Sold for £6,800 in 2001

ILLUSTRATIONS

Other talent went into graphic design and book illustration. This was seldom intended for the wall and never exhibited, so some of the best practitioners remain unlisted and unknown, but perhaps worth seeking out and collecting. There are notable exceptions: E. H. Shepard springs to mind. You will have to pay around £70,000 now for an original illustration for *Winnie The Pooh*, so avoid him.

LIVING ARTISTS

You may want to consider living artists. The rewards, if you back the right horse, can be astounding. If you had bought an early Damien Hirst for a few hundred pounds, it would be worth hundreds of thousands now. But how could you have known? Nothing in an artist's work at his career's outset may give the least clue to his future celebrity. There is no substitute for meeting the artist, and discussing his pictures with him. You quickly get an idea of his sincerity, and you may understand his pictures much better than at first glance or through the explanations of an interlocutor. I met Tobit Roche socially at first, for instance, and only gradually understood what a good painter he is.

You could buy pictures by subject – there are some good animal painters around. Take James Lynch, for example. You could have bought a work of his in the 1980s for £1,500 that would cost you £8,500 now.

Where to search depends on your budget and time available. If you have less money and more time, then look round country auctions, flea markets and the north end of Portobello Road (cheaper than the south). Look out for new young talent at the London art schools' degree shows in June. For those with more to spend, art fairs are the best places to observe dealers, and to view their stock without obligation, the better to assess whether you would like to meet them or to do business with them.

Resources

Further reading

British Art Since 1900, Frances Spalding, Thames & Hudson, 1986

A Concise History of Modern Painting, Sir Herbert Read, Thames and Hudson, 1974

The Nature of Light and Colour in the Open Air, M. Minnaert, Dover Publications, 1954

Internet sites

www.artnet.com
Selections from stock of top dealers. The research area, to which you can subscribe, gives images, details and prices for auction art sales.

www.art-sales-index.com
Gives the raw data only, no images but less expensive to use.

www.antiquestradegazette.co.uk
Internet presence of the British trade newspaper, it lists all auctions countrywide on a weekly basis.

www.bridgeman.co.uk
A good, easily searchable site of images to learn from

Art fairs and exhibitions

20/21 British Art Fair (in September at the Royal College of Art)
T: 020 8742 1611   www.britishartfair.co.uk

The Affordable Art Fair (Two a year in London, one in Bristol)
T: 020 7371 8787   www.affordableartfair.co.uk

The Grosvenor House Art and Antiques Fair, London W1
T: 020 7399 8100   www.grosvenor-antiquesfair.co.uk

The Watercolours and Drawings Fair (late January/early February at the Park Lane Hotel in London)
T: 01798 861815   www.watercoloursfair.com

Camberwell, City & Guilds Art School, London SE11
T: 020 7735 2306/5210   www.cityandguildsartschool.ac.uk

Central Saint Martins College of Art & Design, London WC1
T: 020 7514 7000   www.csm.linst.ac.uk

The Royal Academy of Arts (Summer exhibition each June), London W1   T: 020 7300 8000   www.royalacademy.org.uk

Dealers

Abbott and Holder, London WC1
T: 020 7637 3981   www.abbottandholder.co.uk

Jonathan Clark & Co, London SW10
T: 020 7351 3555   www.jonathanclarkfineart.com

Julian Hartnoll, London SW1   T: 020 7839 3842

The Maas Gallery, London W1
T: 020 7734 2302   www.maasgallery.com

The Black Bottle, Samuel John Peploe, RSA, 1871–1935. Oil on canvas.
Signed. 20 x 30 in. Sold for £470,000 in 2001

TIMELINE

Samuel John Peploe's oil *The Black Bottle* was worth about £120 in 1910. It stayed at that value without appreciating at all until about 1980, when it would have been worth £6,500. In 1988, it sold for £260,000 and in 2001 for £470,000. It must be worth well over £650,000 now.

CRYSTAL BALL

Look out for illustrations to well-remembered books of your own childhood – the Ladybird books, perhaps? The rule with this kind of art is that if it is very much of its time, and, of course, well executed, then it is probably worth buying and is likely to gain value in the future.

Mother Has Bought A New Hat, 1966, Martin Aitchison. Gouache on board.
10½ x 7½ in. *The Big House Book 8b*, The Ladybird Key Words Reading Scheme

INDEX